GOOD ROOTS

WRITERS REFLECT ON GROWING UP IN OHIO

Edited by Lisa Watts

Ohio University Press   Athens

Grateful acknowledgment is made to the following publications where these pieces first appeared, some in slightly different form:

Jill Bialosky: "Fathers in the Snow," from *The End of Desire: Poems* by Jill Bialosky, copyright © 1997 by Jill Bialosky, and "Terminal Tower," from *Subterranean: Poems* by Jill Bialosky, copyright © 2001 by Jill Bialosky. Used by permission of Alfred A. Knopf, a division of Random House, Inc.

Michael Dirda: "Sweet Lorain," *Preservation,* January/February 2000.

Rita Dove: "The Buckeye" and "The Gorge," from *Grace Notes,* copyright © 1989 by Rita Dove. Used by permission of the author and W. W. Norton and Company, Inc.; "Wingfoot Lake," from *Thomas and Beulah,* Carnegie-Mellon University Press, © 1986 by Rita Dove, reprinted by permission of the author.

Ian Frazier: "Out of Ohio," *New Yorker,* January 10, 2005.

Mary Oliver: "Answers," "Spring in the Classroom," reprinted with permission by the author; "The Black Walnut Tree," reprinted with permission from Little, Brown.

Susan Orlean: "Pool Buddy," *New Yorker,* June 22, 1998.

Julie Salamon: "This Is the Place," from *Net of Dreams* (Random House, 1998).

Scott Russell Sanders: "After the Flood," from *Staying Put: Making a Home in a Restless World,* by Scott Russell Sanders, copyright © 1993 by Scott Russell Sanders, reprinted by permission of Beacon Press, Boston.

Alix Kates Shulman: parts of her piece first appeared in "Alix Kates Shulman Talks about Her New Memoir, *A Good Enough Daughter,*" *Ohioana Quarterly,* Spring 1999.

Jeffery Smith: from *Where the Roots Reach for Water: A Personal and Natural History of Melancholia* (Farrar, Straus and Giroux, 1999).

Mark Winegardner: from introduction to *We Are What We Ate: 24 Memories of Food* (Harvest Books, 1998).

Ohio University Press, Athens, Ohio 45701
www.ohio.edu/oupress
© 2007 by Ohio University Press

Printed in the United States of America
All rights reserved

14 13 12 11 10 09 08 07   5 4 3 2 1

Library of Congress Cataloging-in-Publication Data

Good roots : writers reflect on growing up in Ohio / edited by Lisa Watts.
  p. cm.
Includes bibliographical references.
ISBN-13: 978-0-8214-1728-7 (cloth : alk. paper)
ISBN-10: 0-8214-1728-2 (cloth : alk. paper)
ISBN-13: 978-0-8214-1729-4 (pbk. : alk. paper)
ISBN-10: 0-8214-1729-0 (pbk. : alk. paper)
  1. Authors, American—Homes and haunts—Ohio. 2. Authors, American—20th century—Biography. I. Watts, Lisa, 1960–
PS571.O3G66 2007
810.9'32759—dc22
[B]
                                                                2006030138

To Kate and Tommy,
may your Ohio roots help you thrive
wherever you choose to plant yourselves.

Contents

In Fields and Woods

Acknowledgments

Dale Keiger won't remember this, but he first planted the seed of this collection a few years ago when I ran into him at the Galleria Mall in Cambridge, Massachusetts. We were both killing time before the start of our annual college editors' conference. Wide-eyed, I told Dale we didn't have malls like this—with whole stores devoted to such things as Macintosh computers and cell phones—back in Ohio. He laughed and said he understood because he had grown up in Mt. Healthy, outside Cincinnati.

When the bookstore at that same mall featured a display of books by poet Mary Oliver, a native of Maple Heights, and *New Yorker* writer Susan Orlean mentioned as an aside during her keynote talk that she grew up in Ohio, something clicked.

This collection of writers whom I admire and who share Buckeye roots grew from there. Thanks to all of you for opening my e-mail or letter just because the title line said, "about Ohio." It has been an honor to correspond with such talented and successful writers. A whole shelf in my office, my "Ohio shelf," is stuffed with your books. And thanks to R. L. Stine, who wrote his foreword just days after he finished another book. In my kids' eyes, this book now includes a "real" writer.

I met Dan Cryer, a freelance writer and book reviewer, when I was editing his alumni magazine in Wooster. Dan was a great help in suggesting more writers to include in this collection. He even served as an intermediary when Tony Doerr and I couldn't receive each other's e-mails. Thank you to Barbara Meister, librarian at Ohioana Library, who also helped me reach a few of these writers; and thanks to Melody Snure, my first Ohio employer, who connected me with Barbara.

Jimmy Meyer, your ear and copyeditor's eye are always appreciated. Susan Stranahan, your enthusiasm right from the start helped me stay on track. Likewise, my sister Sandy, of all my siblings, truly cherishes her Cleveland Heights childhood and really rooted for this collection.

I will always remember that first encouraging phone call from Gillian Berchowitz, senior editor at Ohio University Press, just days after I sent her a proposal for this book. Last winter she handed the project to David Sanders, the Press's director and a native Ohioan. David's e-mails and phone calls have been a great treat—supportive, thoughtful, and respectful.

And to Bob Malekoff, who thinks his name isn't appearing anywhere in this book, here you go. Thanks for the space you gave me to undertake this project; it's one of the best gifts a husband can give a wife.

Goofy Ohio Stories and Other Sweet Things

R. L. Stine

"Did you have a *scary* childhood?"

Because I write scary books, kids always ask me that question. And I have to disappoint them by saying, "No, I had a very normal, uneventful childhood." The Columbus suburb I grew up in was quiet and pretty and nurturing.

The truth is, it didn't really matter *where* I spent my childhood. I discovered an old typewriter when I was eight or nine and dragged it into my room to type endless joke magazines and stories. And I was gone, vanished into a world of my own.

I can still hear my mother, standing outside my bedroom door: "Go outside and play. What's *wrong* with you? Go outside and get some fresh air."

My reply: "No. It's BORING out there!" Type type type type.

Would I have ventured outside more if it wasn't so BORING out there? If I lived in a more stimulating, crowded, cosmopolitan, lots-to-see-and-do environment? I don't know. But the quiet and normalcy of my little block of our little town gave me the security to stay inside and explore this new passion of mine.

Many years later, like many of the writers in this book, I live in New York City, where there's more to do and see every day than I could have imagined. Of course, I'm still in my room typing away. But I know it's all outside my window—something for every interest, no matter how particular or personal.

When I was a kid in Columbus in the 1950s, there were eight radio stations in town. And on Saturday afternoons in the fall, *all eight* stations carried the Ohio State football games. Eight different broadcast booths, eight different sets of announcers—and *nothing else* to listen to on the dial.

At the age of eight or nine, I didn't think anything was strange about this.

Today, I tell it as a story about how goofy my hometown was back then—how small-town and provincial, and gung-ho, and "All-American." But, of course, it's more than that. The radio homogeneity shows a kind of unity, of community togetherness that has long disappeared in American life.

Do I miss it? Sometimes. My wife, a native New Yorker, often says, "You'll be from Ohio for the rest of your life." She usually offers that after I've said something naïve or done something really unsophisticated. I don't get insulted. I know it's true.

A few years ago, I returned to Columbus to speak at the elementary schools I attended.

I pulled open the door to the first school and stepped inside. Almost immediately, I heard someone shouting, "Bobby! Bobby!" (No one had called me Bobby in at least forty years!)

I spun around and saw an old, old woman, white hair flying behind her, rushing at me, arms outstretched. "Bobby! Bobby!" She flung herself at me, nearly tackling me to the floor. "Bobby! Don't you recognize me?"

It was my kindergarten teacher. Miss Barbara. At least one hundred and fifty years old. I had to peel her off me. "Bobby, look what I brought." She pulled out a class picture. My kindergarten class picture. I was in kindergarten so long ago, it wasn't a photo—it was a Currier and Ives etching.

We went into the auditorium so that I could speak to the school and tell my scary ghost stories to the kids. But Miss Barbara was introduced before I was.

She stood up and announced, "He's not R. L. to me! He'll always be MY BOBBY!"

And then I had to go out onstage—I had to follow that—and try to be *scary!*

Remembering this awkward, crazy moment with Miss Barbara still makes me laugh. It's another goofy Ohio story I tell people. And for me, aside from being embarrassing, it has a sweetness about it. Because even though it happened just a few years ago, it isn't of this time. It's from a time when teachers remembered every student—even forty years later!—and thought of them as *their* children.

The authors in this book are so diverse. But I'm sure they all have similar stories. Their stories of growing up in Ohio may be funny or embarrassing or frustrating or even angry. But I'm sure they also have that special sweetness about them—because our childhood memories are of a place that doesn't really exist any longer.

about the author

R. L. Stine is the best-selling children's author in history, beginning with his *Goosebumps* series in the early 1990s and followed by his *Fear Street* series. He lives in New York City.

Looking for Roots

Lisa Watts

My thirteen-year-old son gets it. We are driving on the outskirts of Greensboro, North Carolina, our new home, and he is puzzling over state character along with every other part of his identity. "People make fun of Ohio, like it's so 'country' or something," Tommy says. "But you could make fun of North Carolina, too."

I know what he means. In the last few months, whenever we told someone we were leaving Ohio to move to North Carolina, they would tell us, "Oh, it's so beautiful there," or "You're going to love the weather." Yet here we are suffocating in the swelter of a mid-August North Carolina heat wave, and we remember beauty—the rolling hills of farm country dotted with hay bales outside our small Ohio town, or the way a sunset lit the entire downtown sky, leaving the city hall tower in silhouette.

And "country," as in unsophisticated? We have heard southern accents in Greensboro so thick that we can't make out the words. We have driven down some sad streets dotted with pawnshops and dollar stores.

In truth, it is pretty in our new home, and the heat will ease in September. We're all just a little out of sorts. For both of my kids, Ohio has just become the place where they're from, where they grew up. They lived there for almost ten years and had no reason to believe they would leave their comfortable small-town existence until they chose to, for college or work. Now their dad has found a new job and we've plopped them down in a southern city, promising them more things to do, less small-town nosiness, more opportunity. But I know what Tommy and his sister, Kate, are thinking. *We liked it in Ohio. They do have running water there, you know. Why do people make fun of it?*

I am the cheerleader, the one in our family who embraces change. Yet even I am grieving what we've lost, part of which is my kids' sense of roots.

ONE COMMON THREAD GATHERS the writers collected in *Good Roots:* they all grew up in Ohio. Their childhoods were as varied as their work, even as the state itself. Poets, novelists, reporters, essayists, they lived in the cities of Cleveland, Akron, and Cincinnati or in small towns. Others knew a rural Ohio of county townships. Yet what each tells us about roots, about growing up a Buckeye, resonates as a whole, building a shared sense of heritage.

Some people suggest that Ohio is too varied to claim a true sense of place. Clevelanders probably share more in common with someone in Erie, Pennsylvania, say, than with a southern Ohioan. Northern Ohio moves west from the lake-effect snowbelt to the flat plains and gridded streets of Toledo. Much of central Ohio remains agricultural, with rolling fields bounded by high ridges and new housing developments. Columbus and Cincinnati grow like trumpet vine, their suburbs creeping farther into the country. In southern Ohio, extended families travel back and forth across the Ohio River to Kentucky and West Virginia.

Yet Ohioans must share more than just the same license plate and tax address. Politicians eye us as a swing state, a piece of Middle America that makes up its political mind depending on the economy and other down-to-earth concerns. Some think of the state as the last holdout for innocence, a place where Norman Rockwell scenes can be found even on the streets of our most sophisticated cities.

New Yorker writer Ian Frazier suggests, in his introduction to *Best American Travel Writing 2003,* that Ohio is a place from which people leave. "When I was growing up there, Ohio seemed centrifugal. Some mystical force the place possessed flung people from it, often far." Leaving in itself can form a bond. Frazier marvels at the time when, halfway around the world and walking through a Moroccan market, he met a man from Cincinnati.

Leaving also unites the writers in this anthology. To a person, they have moved away from their home state. Many were drawn to New York City, even if they've since left that literary capital to raise families: Frazier and his *New Yorker* colleague Susan Orlean, Andrea Louie, P. J. O'Rourke,

Alix Kates Shulman. Others have settled on the coasts, from poet Mary Oliver on Cape Cod to nature writer Kathleen Dean Moore in Oregon. Some, like Elizabeth Dodd in Kansas and Scott Russell Sanders in Indiana, have learned to call other parts of the Midwest home, to trade hardwood forest for prairie grass, as Dodd says.

Clearly their Ohio roots haven't hurt these writers. Their collective résumé reads like a literary Who's Who, including four Pulitzer Prizes, a few National Book Awards, and many prestigious fellowships. They were among my favorite writers long before I knew of their birthplaces. Each addition to the list, another writer we could "claim," boosted our shared pride, as if we were alumni learning of another successful classmate.

Does it mean something that so many successful writers come from Ohio? Perhaps. These contemporary scribes follow in the footsteps of many Buckeyes before them—poet James Wright (1927–80), for one. After growing up in Martins Ferry, Wright traveled the world and earned an impressive collection of awards and fellowships, including a Pulitzer in 1978. Humorist James Thurber (1894–1961) is a favorite son of Columbus, where one of his childhood homes now serves as a literary center. The books of conservationist Louis Bromfield (1896–1956) made famous his Malabar Farm near Mansfield. Around the same time, Sherwood Anderson (1876–1941) drew on his childhood in Clyde, Ohio, for his book *Winesburg, Ohio*. Langston Hughes (1902–67) was named class poet at Cleveland's Central High.

It's a rich literary tradition, but it's a quiet one. Ohioans aren't much for blowing their own horns. We suffer a low-level inferiority complex, caught in the middle as we are—Ohio isn't quite east enough to be East Coast, north enough to fit in with Michigan, south enough to be genteel, or west enough to be the true heartland. We know that Ohio doesn't show up on many lists for top 10 vacation spots. We're well aware that most people living on either coast couldn't pick our state out from Iowa or Wisconsin. And we're all too familiar with gray clouds hanging over the northern half of our little piece of the Midwest from November until April.

A pervasive lack of pretension, so noticeable to anyone arriving from the coasts, probably strengthens creative souls here. This is a state, after all, where we call the weathered "Chew Mail Pouch Tobacco" ads that adorn our barns art. Maybe by not taking ourselves too seriously, Ohioans open the door to producing serious work. Perhaps there really is a certain innocence here that allows our young people to dream big, not to grow up jaded and cynical. Many of the writers collected here read voraciously in their youth. Few expressed self-doubt about their writing careers; they simply pursued them.

TECHNICALLY I AM A native Ohioan. I was born at the Cleveland Clinic and brought home to join three sisters and a brother in Cleveland Heights. My earliest memory is a sensory one: I recall venturing out after a snowstorm, in my favorite red corduroy pants, with my mother to buy a red pack of Winstons. The snowbanks reached nearly to the top of my head.

But when I was three, our family moved to Atlanta, later to Baltimore, then Boston. I lived most of my life on the East Coast, in various suburban split-levels and colonials. What I know of place, of childhood roots, is the transience of new suburbs and reborn cities. I know the adventure of riding my bike through mazes of construction—around gravel piles, odd scraps of lumber, mud hills—as yet another field or stretch of woods morphed into the newest subdivision.

Not my older sisters, though. They recall a nearly idyllic Cleveland Heights childhood. They tell of Dad flooding the backyard for ice-skating. They remember the freedom of walking to the five-and-dime, the library, art lessons. It seemed the perfect semi-urban environment—the comfort of suburbia blended with the cultural opportunities of a city. They felt rooted in the church, the neighbors, and our grandparents nearby.

I envy that kind of childhood, that sense of home that so many of these writers remember in *Good Roots.* It is what I had hoped to give my own children in the small Ohio town of Wooster. There I found a grounding that I never encountered back east. People grow up in Wooster. Their parents and grandparents live an easy drive away. Some people are just passing through, because this is a college town. Others are leaving as the once vibrant manufacturing industry jumps off the sinking ship that is the Midwest economy. But by and large, you can live in north-central Ohio and surround yourself with Ohioans, people born there and raising their children there.

Good Roots is a tribute to such people, and to Ohio—to its screened porches and gray skies, to its rural towns and gritty cities, to its lack of pretension yet its very real value. In remembering their childhoods, the writers honor another, earlier time, but they also honor a place. It's one that many of us cherish, even if we can't still call it home.

City Sensibilities

So maybe nobody ever confused downtown Cleveland with Manhattan or Chicago. Writers such as Alix Kates Shulman and Jill Bialosky still managed to find great allure in their native city. The rapid-transit train that whisked fathers from Shaker and Cleveland Heights to offices downtown could also transport young teenagers sneaking off for a day of adventure among the department stores and lunch shops in the shadow of the Terminal Tower.

Rita Dove remembers Akron as a small-town city segregated by color yet united by big employers like Goodyear, where family members might work for their entire careers. Indeed, from Akron's tire plants to the steel mills and factories dotting Cleveland and Cincinnati, Columbus and Youngstown, Ohio's cities of the 1950s and '60s were places where things got made and families prospered.

P. J. O'Rourke and Michael Dirda recognize the uniquely midwestern flavor of their hometowns, Toledo and Lorain. These smaller cities also were home to mills and factories, drawing migrants from Europe and beyond who quickly set to work becoming Americans. Having gone to school with the hardworking Irish and Polish, Germans and Czechs, both men recognize the values instilled by an industrial culture, what Dirda calls a "sturdy, honest world."

Those who fall in love with city life say its greatest charms are found in the small worlds which one creates out of daily patterns—the bagel shop guy who knows your order, the elderly couple who stop to chat with your dog. In the midst of a vast, anonymous place, life takes on some comforting familiarity. In that way, maybe Manhattan takes its lessons from Cleveland and Lorain, from Toledo and Akron.

Fathers in the Snow

and other selected poems

Jill Bialosky

SHAKER HEIGHTS

Jill Bialosky (in stroller) takes a walk with sister Laura and her parents

Fathers in the Snow

In memory of Milton Abraham Bialosky

1.

The game is called *father.*

My sister lies in the grass.
I take handfuls of leaves
we raked from the lawn
spilling them over her body

until she's buried—

her red jacket lost, completely.
Then it's my turn.

Afterwards, we pick the brittle pieces
from each other's hair.

2.

After father died
the love was all through the house
untamed and sometimes violent.
When the dates came we went up to our rooms
and mother entertained.
Frank Sinatra's "Strangers in the Night,"
the smell of Chanel No. 5 in her hair and the laughter.
We sat crouched at the top of the stairs.
In the morning we found mother asleep on the couch
her hair messed, and the smell
of stale liquor in the room.
We knelt on the floor before her,
one by one touched our fingers
over the red flush in her face.

The chipped sunlight through the shutters.
It was a dark continent
we and mother shared;
it was sweet and lonesome,
the wake men left in our house.

5.

When the lightning
struck we were sure the dark limbs would splinter
but instead the tree was all light
and beautiful.
The tree long ago had been transformed,
had become for us, our father.

For days after the storm
we guarded its dark secret.
There were no blessings
large enough for that body
wrapped in weathered bark.

The day the men came
to cut down our tree
we had said them all:
One sister rubbed
her doll's face with mud
that covered the twisted roots,
the other sister hammered
her fist against the bark.

I carried a last leaf
in my pocket for luck.

6.

I come home
to the white framed house,

the paint on the side peeling
as if grieving for something lost

and the yellow forsythia tree
grown wild in the backyard
letting go its closed blossoms.

By the side door
is the milk chute.
we crawled through
nights locked out of the house.

And in the backyard,
the stump of our oak tree
standing like a headstone
in the middle of the dried lawn.
Once its broken limbs protected our roof.

Indoors mother sleeps
all day on her double bed
while dandelions work their way
through the torn-up grass.

9.

It was the light of day
dispersing, the white light
of my mother's skin
and the light of her love
sparkling in the snow.
From the window
I saw her playing solitaire.
I had watched her play
so many nights
from outside I could feel
each card slapped down.

There was no escape
from the rash of her loss:
it was the cold rusty
taste of snow
I licked off my mitten;
the chill down my spine
when my sister
put her snow-filled hand
under my coat
the other sister
holding me down;
it was those long dark shadows
I believed looked after us,
gigantic in the snow.

10.

Years ago I found them
scattered like dead leaves
in a suitcase in the basement:
the pictures of my father.

I took the best ones
time hadn't reached
and opened the edges
curled like a hand.

I put them in a shoe-box,
slipped under my bed.
It was like a secret
I imagined we shared.

Eventually the tint of age
faded the images,
erased the details.
Even my hands forgot you.

Terminal Tower

From the top of the tower when the sun set in the Cuyahoga's
    brown waters
(the river that caught fire and made our city the laughingstock of
    a nation)
it cast a dark shadow over the industrial sky.
To the Van Sweringen brothers it was like the Eiffel Tower of Paris
conceived in 1925 like a favorite child in a family—it foreshadowed
Rockefeller Center and gave to our city the second-tallest
    building—
to us it was as grand as Mount Olympus.
It was the place we imagined Zeus and his cronies conducted
their mortal business. There is a legend about a lost daughter
and a mother who must bargain for her return. Weren't we all
    lost
inside our daydreams and imaginings?
Didn't all of us who lived off the shores of Lake Erie want to be
    claimed?
On an overcast day you can still make out the intricate masonry
    of its patrician face.
It was where the fathers of our community worked, riding the
    rapid transit
from the safe suburbs through the poverty of the ghetto into the
    underbelly
of downtown. When we looked from the ground to the top of
    the tower
we felt our spirits elevate. Then I heard it, inside the crowds, the
    honking
of automobiles and shriek of an ambulance, the singular cry,
and he was there in all his omnipotence and I knew my fate was
    locked
inside the mortar of his mercurial façade like wet leaves pressed
into a mosaic on the pavement. In synagogue we learned

about Moses climbing the mount and God's deliverance
of the commandments. Whether the sound came from a
    wounded gull
or a school of dirty pigeons did not matter. Whether it was
    Zeus or God
the Almighty or my own vision of my lost father was irrelevant.
It was the idea of being greater than myself I coveted. It *was*
    terminal,
the longing. It *was* magnificent, a tower that did not look desolate
in its setting, a structure to provide an anchor to the observer's
    glance, a relief from the flatness of the world around us.
In the tower's square men clad in overcoats carrying briefcases
trafficked the street, rode its fifty-two floors to politick. And it
    was at the very top
where Zeus might have bargained with the prince of the
    underworld
for his daughter's return. As I looked up the sweep of the tower's
    long elegance,
I saw through a mass of smog that I might lose myself forever
    or I might survive.
I saw that he was looking after me, but that he was also indifferent.
I saw that love was fickle and adulterous and still I longed for him.
I saw that he betrayed us and that he could not save me.
I saw through the stone into the abyss. It was dark and splendid.

The Poet Returns Home for the Holidays

We entered the city
and even the son said it was small, all the houses one size
not the skyscrapers and mass of mayhem,
the streams of people he was used to.
I love this city of my birth with all the ornaments and lights,
the nativity scenes on the lawns, the colors of red, white, and green
to please the passersby in their cars, the simple life:
dinners at home, hockey games, lunch at the skating club,
whole days spent in libraries reading the papers.
So many memories unleashed like bats escaping from the light.
When I read my poems at the bookstore on the square
to friends and neighbors with their good and true hearts,
I wondered what they thought, the way I looked
beneath the surface to find the grit, where the trees
are fragile, the streets whole avenues of loss,
the places no one wants to go to; the sun slipping
through the cracks.
It was so strange they did not want to see what I saw.

PHOTO BY MARION ETTINGER

about the author

JILL BIALOSKY is the author of two poetry collections, *The End of Desire* (Alfred A. Knopf) and *Subterranean* (Alfred A. Knopf), which was a finalist for the James Laughlin Prize from the Academy of American Poets. She coedited, with Helen Schulman, *Wanting a Child* (Farrar, Straus and Giroux). In 2002 she published her first novel, *House under Snow* (Harcourt). Her poems and essays have appeared in the *New Yorker,* the *Nation, Redbook, O Magazine, Partisan Review,* the *Antioch Review,* the *New Republic,* the *Paris Review, Poetry, American Poetry Review, TriQuarterly,* and the *Kenyon Review.*

Bialosky is an executive editor and vice president at W. W. Norton and Company and lives in New York City.

Sweet Lorain

Michael Dirda

LORAIN

Michael Dirda, second from left, and his oldest sister, Sandra (on bike), with next-door neighbors
(© 2003 Chester Simpson)

EVEN NOW, WHEN I HAVEN'T LIVED
in Lorain for more than thirty years, I still think of it not only as home
but also as a strangely magical place. Isn't there, after all, a kind of Iron
Age romance to deteriorating industrial towns? Eyes closed, I see the
puffing smokestacks of National Tube, the slag heaps guarding Black
River, those ponderous lake freighters cautiously docking near the jackknife bridge, and, of course, Lake View Park, with its antiaircraft guns,
rose garden, and giant Easter basket, all on the eroding shores of the blue
and polluted Erie. Even now, I can feel the bumpy B&O railroad tracks
crossing Oberlin Avenue, touch the soft accumulation of grit on cars
parked along Pearl Avenue, taste the cherry vanilla at the long-gone Home
Dairy ice cream company. So many places linger in the memory—St.
Stanislaus Church, where Polish fishermen attended 5:00 a.m. Mass, the
Czech Grill, the Abruzzi Club, the Slovak Hall, Pulaski Park. Who can
doubt that I grew up in what sociologists would quickly label "a classic
midwestern Rust Belt city"?

Sweet Lorain, as poet Bruce Weigl called it in his recent book of
poems. Nobel Prize winner Toni Morrison was born and educated there,
and so was General Johnnie Wilson, the highest-ranking African American in the U.S. military until his retirement. Comedian Don Novello,
a.k.a. Father Guido Sarducci, grew up there. My high school was named
after favorite son Admiral Ernest J. King, commander of the fleet
during World War II. It was rumored that Admiral King High School
boasted—le mot juste—the highest rate of juvenile delinquency in the
state. Might well have been true, since many of my classmates belonged
to "clubs" such as Bachelors, Dukes, Barons, Cavaliers, Southerners (de-
noting South Lorain), Islets, Stylers (for guys with a particular interest
in souped-up cars), and Bishops (black kids only). There were girl gangs,
too—Emeralds, Rainbows, Junior Gems. And at least a third of AKHS
was African American or Hispanic: following the Second World War,
U.S. Steel had recruited five hundred Puerto Ricans to come work at
National Tube. Need I say that we fielded powerhouse football and basketball teams? Go Admirals!

"Industrial Empire in Ohio's Vacationland"—so proclaimed a sign
as one entered the Lorain city limits. It's not there anymore. I suppose
the local solons realized how ludicrous it must have seemed after Thew

Shovel moved away and American Shipbuilding shut down and Japan's Kobe Steel bought National Tube, reducing a work force of thirteen thousand to two thousand, and Lake Erie was declared unsafe for bathing and its perch and white bass too dangerous to eat.

But, amazingly, Lorain seems to have survived. As Ohio's "International City," it still has a festival each year, with an international princess and a fair where one can eat kielbasa and pierogi and souvlaki and tacos and cannoli. One year booths sold T-shirts emblazoned with your choice of ethnic heritage: "I'm Polish and Proud," "I'm Italian and Proud," "I'm Mexican and Proud." Little wonder that I was at least twelve before it dawned on me that not everyone in the world was Catholic.

Almost everybody's father was a laborer, putting in long, sweaty hours on the line at the Ford Assembly Plant or down at the mill, as National Tube was called. Many men worked turns, seven to three one week, three to eleven the next, eleven to seven following that—and most leaped at the chance to earn time-and-a-half for an extra four or eight hours. During a couple of summers I suffered through a grinding routine like this, one year as a bricklayer's helper relining vessels and furnaces, another as a laborer in the rolling mill. Everyone knows that steel mills are volcanically hot and perilous, but you have no idea how deafening they are when behemoth machinery is hammering gigantic ingots into long, round pipes. And the air! Sometimes I could see graphite particles gently floating around me, and would wade through half an inch of fine gray dust on a floor that had been swept clean eight hours before. At other times I used to work in tunnels underground, in a crepuscular half-light, shoveling up loose slabs of ore—the outside scale that had fallen from cooling ingots—and then upend my loaded wheelbarrow into buckets the size of conversion vans, which would be hauled away by distant overhead cranes. Laved with sweat trapped inside green asbestos clothing, often wearing a respirator to protect my lungs, I would occasionally stumble across a mentally retarded coworker sitting in the dark behind a mound of slag, talking excitedly to imaginary companions. For one memorable week, in this realm of Moloch, I even debated election and damnation with a young born-again fundamentalist who had dreams of going to Bible college.

To me, it was all overpowering, awesome, even sublime—but I knew I wouldn't be spending my life there, as my father had and his father before him. Yet sometimes, at two or three in the morning, I'd find myself high up in 4-seamless or one of the other sections of the plant, and I'd look out at the stacks with their flaming gases, smell the rotten-egg odor of the pickling vats, and survey the Piranesi-like ramparts and ladders and rusting buildings. One felt like Satan surveying the immeasurable expanse of hell. What better place, I thought, to argue about free will and the afterlife?

For religion was important in Lorain, which had once been called Ohio's "city of churches." In the summer there were church picnics, with Tilt-A-Whirls, raffles, and seared pigs or sheep slowly roasting on revolving spits. One day a year the priest would come to bless your house, accept a cup of coffee, and taste your nut roll. Sad-eyed ladies of the Altar Society would clean and decorate for holy days. Serious children, in ill-fitting suits or pretty, ruffled white dresses, would march in processions to receive their first Holy Communion, or the Knights of Columbus would parade in uniform and salute with uplifted swords. Someone would always faint during midnight mass, finally overcome by the incense. Naturally, there were fish fries on Friday at the K of C hall. On Ash Wednesday half the townspeople sported gray smudges on their foreheads. At Christmas families would gather at the union headquarters—the AFL-CIO—and hear rousing speeches, especially if a strike threatened, then sing carols and line up to receive a special gift from Santa.

In the evenings one might go shopping downtown, already starting to decay by the mid-1960s, and buy some Faroh's chocolates or stop at the Ohio, Tivoli, or Palace for a movie. Back in the 1920s a tornado had touched down one Saturday afternoon, killing fifteen moviegoers at the State, as the Palace was then called. Those who survived would talk about it all their lives. Out at the first big shopping center, called O'Neill's after its department store, year after year one could chat with a gigantic talking Christmas tree. Afterward, a father might drive his wife and sleepy children around the town so that they could ooh and ah at all the lights and decorations.

At holidays mothers would cook all morning and take stuffed cabbage or lechvar cookies on afternoon social calls that would sometimes last into the evening. Uncles would drink shots and beers, grow jovial, then start dealing poker around a kitchen table. Little kids would play tag or hide-and-seek, teenagers might flirt, and I, a bookish little boy, would plop down in a corner and read about Tarzan while munching on a ham sandwich with sweet pickles, as happy as I will ever be. Sometimes my Uncle Henry would take out his battered concertina and we would all dance or pretend to dance in his kitchen. At other enchanted times, an older cousin might show off his new bow or .22 rifle, and even allow a four-eyed pipsqueak to sight down its smooth, black barrel.

To wander around Lorain was always an adventure. A kid could climb on his bike and cover the entire town in a single summer afternoon. You might start by pedaling up to the shanty in Central Park, where you could sign out basketballs, checkerboards, and frames for weaving potholders or lanyards. Then you might race up to Hawthorne Junior High, where I once received not one but two black eyes in a street fight with a kid named Andy. Then over to Broadway, past the Music Center, where we all took accordion lessons, and up toward Rusine's cigar store, where you could buy racy paperbacks wrapped in cellophane, and on to Cane's Surplus, where a boy might admire the folding slingshots and stilettos. By crossing the jackknife bridge to the East Side you could swing by the shipyards and then take the long vertiginous span of the 21st Street bridge and peer down at the inky water of the river or across to the mountains of slag and coke. Afterward you might turn up 28th Street, lined with ethnic bars, tailor and shoe-repair shops, and mom-and-pop eateries.

If you went far enough, traveling under the rail overpass, you'd ride into South Lorain, up to the aging YMCA, a monumental red-brick building. From near there you could sometimes glimpse elephantine Euclid trucks lumbering around inside the mill, but before long you'd probably set out for Pearl Avenue to stop at Clarice's Values, the apotheosis of all possible junk shops, from which Clarice herself would sell you, for a mere fifty cents, all the books you could carry away. Then past St. Vitus Church, where we played on the steps before Saturday catechism class, on to dilapidated Oakwood shopping center, and then, probably, a turn down one of the graveled side roads.

On one lived my Uncle Steve and Aunt Anna, on another Uncle Henry and Aunt Alice. This latter house gloried in a paradise of rusting steel—old cars, broken engines, metal barrels, bundles of wire—and a chicken shed and a park-sized swing set. In the summers I would visit my slightly older cousin Henry, and we would trudge up to the railroad tracks a quarter mile away and bring back, in wooden wheelbarrows, hunks of coal, scraps of lumber, or even lengths of railroad tie for my uncle's wood-burning furnace. In exchange, he would disburse a nickel pack of BBs for each load—at least until this foolish soul plinked out the street light in front of the house. It was a particularly important light because it helped illuminate the grassy corner lot where half the neighborhood would assemble for softball games on soft summer nights.

Does all this sound idyllic? Well, it should. Bliss was it in Lorain to be alive, but to be young was very heaven. Even adolescence was intermittently endurable. Playing cards on Friday evenings in Lethargy Hall, as we called my friend Ray's basement; cruising up and down Broadway in our friend Tom's 1964 GTO, L'il Blue Tiger; necking ecstatically in Lake View Park with a Saturday night date—how could anyone better spend the confused and angst-ridden years of high school? All around my friends and me the great world hummed, but Lorain remained its own place, homey and human-scaled, living for football games at George Daniel Field and carnivals at shopping centers and parades on the Fourth of July and long, slow beers, sipped by tired steelworkers, slouching in Adirondack chairs in oak-tree-shaded backyards.

Certainly, I mythologize. Perhaps more than a bit. Childhood can be a golden age no matter where it is spent. And yet Toni Morrison regularly goes back to Lorain and in interviews expresses a similar affection for the place. Fifteen or more years ago, Gloria Emerson contributed an article about the city to *Vanity Fair* and later told me how much she envied anyone who could grow up in such a sturdy, honest world. And, of course, I return there still, to see my widowed mother and my sisters. My own children spend part of their summers in Lorain with their cousins, wonderful days of baseball and hide-and-seek and swimming, and at the end of every visit they always say to me, "Dad, why can't we live in Lorain? Why do we have to go back to stupid, dull Washington?" I never quite know what to tell them. Doubtless their parents would go crazy after a couple of weeks, and obviously I have a job and their mother has a job, and clearly there are a dozen really good reasons not to be in Lorain. But even now I sometimes wonder. Could I go back home, back to this ardently beloved, industrial Eden? Probably not. But like other exiles from paradise, I can still murmur *"Et in Arcadia ego"*—I too have lived in Arcadia.

about the author

A longtime columnist for the *Washington Post Book World*, MICHAEL DIRDA writes chiefly about literature and intellectual history, with a particular interest in literary fiction, children's books, contemporary fantasy, translation, and classics. Besides his reviews, he also contributes occasional features and personal pieces about books and writing, many collected in *Readings: Essays and Literary Entertainments* (Indiana University Press, 2000). Each week he conducts an online discussion called Dirda on Books for washingtonpost.com.

Awarded the Pulitzer Prize for criticism in 1993, Dirda collected some of his longer essays in *Bound to Please* (W. W. Norton, 2004); it ranges from Herodotus and *The Arabian Nights* to Samuel Beckett, A. S. Byatt, and P. G. Wodehouse and includes pieces on Ohioans Dawn Powell and Chester Himes. He recently brought out *Book by Book: Notes on Reading and Life* (Henry Holt, 2006), and is currently finishing *Beyond the Lifetime Reading Plan: The Next 100* (Harcourt, to be published in 2007).

Dirda's memoir, *An Open Book* (W. W. Norton, 2003), builds on his contribution to *Good Roots* and takes him through his first two years at Oberlin College. After Oberlin, Dirda went on to graduate work in medieval studies and European romanticism at Cornell University, where he received a PhD in comparative literature.

Grace Notes

Rita Dove

AKRON

Rita Dove with brother, Tommy, 1955

The Buckeye

We learned about the state tree
in school—its fruit
so useless, so ugly

no one bothered to
commend the smudged trunk
nor the slim leaves shifting

over our heads. Yet
they were a good thing to kick
along gutters

on the way home,
though they stank like
a drunk's piss in the roads

where cars had smashed
them. And in autumn
when the spiny helmets split

open,
there was the bald
seed with its wheat-

colored eye.
We loved
the modest countenance beneath

that leathery cap.
We, too, did not want to leave
our mothers.

We piled them up
for ammunition.
We lay down

with them
among the bruised leaves
so that we could

rise, shining.

The Gorge

I.

Little Cuyahoga's done up left town.
No one saw it leaving.
No one saw it leaving

Though it left a twig or two,
And a snaky line of rotting
Fish, a dead man's shoes,

Gnats, scarred pocket-
Books, a rusted garden nozzle,
Rats and crows. April

In bone and marrow. Soaked
With sugary dogwood, the gorge floats
In the season's morass,

Remembering its walnut, its hickory,
Its oak, its elm,
Its sassafras. Ah,

II.

April's arthritic magnitude!
Little Joe ran away
From the swollen man

On the porch, ran across
The muck to the railroad track.
Lost his penny and sat

Right down by the rail,
There where his father
Couldn't see him crying.

That's why the express
Stayed on the track.
That's why a man

On a porch shouted out
Because his son forgot
His glass of iced water. That's

Why they carried little Joe
Home and why his toe
Ain't never coming back. Oh

III.

This town reeks mercy.
This gorge leaves a trail
Of anecdotes,

The poor man's history.

Wingfoot Lake

(Independence Day, 1964)

On her 36th birthday, Thomas had shown her
her first swimming pool. It had been
his favorite color, exactly—just
so much of it, the swimmers' white arms jutting
into the chevrons of high society.
She had rolled up her window
and told him to drive on, fast.

Now this *act of mercy:* four daughters
dragging her to their husbands' company picnic,
white families on one side and them
on the other, unpacking the same
squeeze bottles of Heinz, the same
waxy beef patties and Salem potato chip bags.
So he was dead for the first time
on Fourth of July—ten years ago

had been harder, waiting for something to happen,
and ten years before that, the girls
like young horses eyeing the track.
Last August she stood alone for hours
in front of the T.V. set
as a crow's wing moved slowly through
the white streets of government.
That brave swimming

scared her, like Joanna saying
Mother, we're Afro-Americans now!
What did she know about Africa?
Were there lakes like this one
with a rowboat pushed under the pier?
Or Thomas' Great Mississippi

with its sullen silks? (There was
the Nile but the Nile belonged

to God.) Where she came from
was the past, 12 miles into town
where nobody had locked their back door,
and Goodyear hadn't begun to dream of a park
under the company symbol, a white foot
sprouting two small wings.

about the author

RITA DOVE once said that her Akron, Ohio, upbringing gave her a midwestern sensibility that "has its feet on the ground but at the same time is looking around with that kind of pioneer spirit." When she envisions a back yard, "it's going to be a midwestern back yard, it's going to be an Akron back yard."

Dove's collections of poetry include *The Yellow House on the Corner* (Carnegie Mellon University Press, 1980), *Museum* (Carnegie Mellon University Press, 1983), *Thomas and Beulah* (Carnegie Mellon University Press, 1986), *Grace Notes* (W. W. Norton, 1989), *Selected Poems* (Vintage, 1993), *Mother Love* (W. W. Norton, 1995), *On the Bus with Rosa Parks* (W. W. Norton, 1999), and *American Smooth* (W. W. Norton, 2004). *Thomas and Beulah*, a collection of interrelated poems loosely based on the life of her grandparents, won the 1987 Pulitzer Prize for poetry, one of many awards and honors Dove has won for her work. She has also published a collection of short stories, *Fifth Sunday* (University of Virginia Press, 1985), and a novel, *Through the Ivory Gate* (Pantheon, 1992), the story of a black woman who returns to Akron, her hometown, as an artist-in-residence at an elementary school.

In 1993 Dove was appointed to a two-year term as poet laureate of the United States; she was the youngest person and the first African American to receive this honor.

Dove is Commonwealth Professor of English at the University of Virginia in Charlottesville, where she lives with her husband, Fred Viebahn, and their daughter, Aviva.

Pool Buddy

Susan Orlean

SHAKER HEIGHTS

Susan Orlean as an Indian squaw, circa 1965

WHEN I WAS IN JUNIOR HIGH SCHOOL,
we spent the whole summer at the pool. The coolest kids had tans in
May; I don't know how they did it. In 1971, when I was fourteen, there
was a kind of bikini that was the absolute butter—a little something
held together at the hips and thorax by brass rings—and early that summer the most popular of the popular girls would pose themselves at pool-
side with the suits twisted a little, so you'd notice the circles of white
skin underneath those rings. I was a redhead with blond eyelashes who
freckled like a banana, and I could never manage a low trick like that. I
sunbathed anyway, and there were a couple of days when I'd actually
turn that sickening purply red in the process and my mom would make
a soda-and-calamine lotion and plaster it on me at night. If you were
lucky, the reward for all that sun was that your hair would get streaks.

There was nothing special about our suburban pool in Shaker
Heights. All summer, we girls lay horizontal, with the sunlight warm and
pinkish on our closed eyes, and absorbed reassuring daily pool sounds:
the shrieking lifeguard whistles, the unaccountable bursts of laughter,
the grumbling PA announcements—"Free swim is over!"—and the
soggy *kshpratshh!* of some fatso doing a last cannonball from the high
board. All summer, we girls gave off two perfumes, subtly intermixed—
the choky smell of chlorine in our hair and Coppertone suntan lotion
everywhere else. Coppertone smelled exactly like coconut daiquiris, only
we didn't know it then.

If you didn't have a summer boyfriend, you had to have a pool buddy.
Going to the pool alone and just being there was too fraught and anxious;
all of us moved in pairs or packs. As the school year wound down, I
would start casting about for my pool partner, covertly comparing
summer-camp schedules and family trips and registering who would be
around and, like me, available. The summer of 1971, Norma Levy was
my pool buddy, and we had a deal. One of us would call the other before heading off to the pool, and the other one had to be ready to leave
at that same instant. Arriving together meant that neither of us ever had
to emerge from the locker room alone, looking blinded and with her
pallid skin glowing geekily. We never wanted to have to hunt around for
a place to sit, or to approach a murmuring group and have no one in it
yield an inch to make room for another towel. Together, Norma and I

were safe. Each could count on the other to push her towel over to make room, and that way, side by side, with our towels touching, we had a raft, a cabana.

We shared our snack-bar money and poured Coppertone onto each other's backs, and we vowed never to ditch the other just because some guy had begun to talk to one of us over by the water fountain and asked her why not come sit with him in the shade. I intended not to do that, but sometimes, on a particularly hot day, when the guy really did have a green towel spread out under the maple tree, up behind the diving boards, I just had to. We all knew that an afternoon date by the pool might not amount to much—might not even amount to a date the next afternoon. Still, it was worth it, even if it meant breaking faith with your pool buddy, because there was no summer moment more perfect than walking off past the diving board alongside someone cute like Randy Ginn and knowing that everyone else at the pool would see. Anyway, I knew Norma would have done it, too, given the chance, so in an instant I said a sheepish goodbye to her and headed off with him, leaving a dark imprint on the concrete where my wet towel had been, knowing that in another instant the sun would fade it away.

about the author

New Yorker writer and literary journalist SUSAN ORLEAN looks at life with a wry humor and an always curious eye. Her book *The Orchid Thief* (Random House, 1998), later the basis of the film *Adaptation*, grew out of a small newspaper story that caught her eye on an airplane trip. Her other books include *My Kind of Place: Travel Stories from a Woman Who's Been Everywhere* (Random House, 2004); *The Bullfighter Checks Her Makeup: My Encounters with Extraordinary People* (Random House, 1987); and *Saturday Night* (Knopf, 1990), a look at how Americans of all ages and regions of the country spend that evening. Her book *Throw Me a Bone* (Simon and Schuster, 2003;

written under the name Cooper Gillespie, her dog) is a cookbook for canines.

Orlean is, she writes, "the product of a happy and relatively uneventful childhood in Cleveland, Ohio, back when the Indians were still a lousy team."

A wife and mother, she splits her time between Boston and New York, along with some time in Columbia County, New York, in a house on a hill with goats and cows for neighbors.

Why It's Good to Come from Nowhere

P. J. O'Rourke

TOLEDO

P. J. (in those days "Pat") O'Rourke with his mother, Delphine; grandmother Olive; dog Sergeant; and sisters (indistinguishably identical twins) Del and Kathy, summer 1962

We're strong for Toledo
T-O-L-E-D-O
Where the boys are the squarest,
The girls are the fairest
Of any old town that I know.

TOLEDO DOESN'T LOOK LIKE MUCH.

And looks do not deceive. Toledo is a coal and grain port, railroad transport junction, auto parts manufacturing center, and, in general, an important hub of industries that aren't so important anymore. It sits at the lower left corner of that runner-up for least great of the Great Lakes, Erie. Toledo is not far from the triple conjunction of the quotidian where the borders of Ohio, Indiana, and Michigan meet. A small concrete post used to mark this spot, and may still. You could balance yourself on the post and experience the very mild thrill of standing, all at once, in Ohio, Indiana, and Michigan. Detroit is fifty-nine miles north of Toledo. Cleveland is one hundred and fifteen miles east. London, Paris, and New York are a million miles away.

Toledo was, last time I checked, the fifty-seventh-largest city in the United States, ranking between Disney-entertained Anaheim, California, and retirement-enjoying Tampa, Florida. At least no one goes to the factories, warehouses, offices, and unemployment lines of Toledo under a wearisome obligation to have fun.

I grew up in Toledo, if "up" is the word. Northwest Ohio is flat. There isn't much up. The land is so flat that a child from Toledo is under the impression that the direction hills go is down. Sledding is done from street level into creek beds and road cuts. Likewise, brave plunges on bicycles, scooters, and cars made from fruit crates and baby carriage wheels. Toledo's tallest building is a modest thirty-two stories. The top-floor windows look out on a supine landscape rising nowhere more than a few dozen feet from the beige and tideless lake. In Toledo, people grow *out*—out to the suburbs, out to the parts of America where the economy is more vigorous, and, all too often, out to a forty-eight-inch waistband size. But no Toledoan would ever say that he or she had "outgrown" Toledo. We are too level-headed for that.

"Level" being the operative term. The world of Toledo is as horizontal as the Great Plains, but without the heroic vistas and infinite distances. There is no horizon in Toledo. There are too many trees. Nor do those trees form the sylvan cathedrals of the North Woods. Dutch elm disease took care of that. Toledo's scenery is brushy and unsublime. True, the Great Lakes, even Erie, are not without romance. The Battle of Put-In Bay was a decisive moment in the history of warfare at sea (or at lake, as it was). But, in a testament to local sensibilities, the battle has a weekend picnic of a name. And the action didn't really take place all that close to Toledo.

When I was young the lake had beaches full of mud and weeds and water full of lampreys and pollution. Sand has since been carted in and sewage carted out. But Lake Erie remains more a source of carp than dreams. There is no twenty-horsepower Evinrude on a leaky rowboat full of live bait like a book.

Toledo sits astride a river. The Maumee is the largest river emptying into the Great Lakes, though unprepossessing for all that. Most times of year it's slow and rather oily. No one has been dipped in the waters of the Maumee and felt his life to be changed (other than by a tetanus shot). There is no Lorelei on the Maumee luring, with her siren song, ships full of soybeans to their destruction on the I-75 abutments. Yet the Maumee, like many an obscure American watercourse, is just large enough—nine hundred feet across as it flows through downtown—to make level-headed tourists from Toledo wonder what is so swell about the Seine or why crossing the Rubicon was ever thought to be a big deal.

Toledo's lack of interesting geography should be offset by its exciting mix of cultures and peoples, but it isn't. The industrial Midwest drew migrants from everywhere in America and the world. Toledo is full of Irish, Poles, Hungarians, southern blacks, and Appalachian whites. There is a large Jewish community and a large Arab community as well. There are so many Germans that a boy I knew, Don Eggenschwiler, went all the way through grade school and junior high without being teased about his name. But no matter what races, religions, or ethnic groups came to Toledo, within months they had aboveground pools, riding lawnmowers, and golf clubs.

Toledoans are true Americans, and it is almost impossible to compel true Americans to be diverse. We're too American. Americans hate foreigners. Americans hate foreigners because Americans *are* foreigners. We all came from strange, outlandish places, even if we came ten thousand years ago on a land bridge across the Bering Strait. We didn't want anything to do with those Ice Age Siberians—them with the itchy cave bearskin underwear and mammoth meat on their breath. We were off for Northwest Ohio with its terrific bluegill fishing, tasty sweet corn, and quarter-acre lots for the wigwam.

Toledoans didn't come to Toledo to be Limeys, Frog-Eaters, Bucketheads, Herring-Chokers, Micks, Spics, or Wogs. If we'd wanted to be foreigners, we would have stayed in foreign countries.

Does the leveling effect of Toledo cause its offspring to eschew lofty goals and higher aspirations? I can only speak for myself. When *The Sound of Music* played in Toledo theaters, I was mystified by the lyrics of "Climb Every Mountain." *Climb every mountain / Search high and low* . . . Low would probably do. *Follow every byway* . . . Toledo is laid out in a rigid, rectangular street grid. *Every path you know* . . . Or ask the guy at the corner gas station. *Climb every mountain* . . . Even though you'd have to spend three days packed in the car with the whole family to get to one. *Ford every stream* . . . Get your foot caught in a discarded snow tire. *Follow every rainbow* . . . And wind up in the middle of a cornfield in Adrian, Michigan.

Triumph has its many paeans. The greatest bards have tuned their lyres for tragedy. But no one sings of the things that didn't quite work out but could have been a lot worse and, come to think of it, really aren't so bad after all.

Nevin O. Winter, an early historian of the Toledo region, wrote in 1917, "It cannot be said that northwest Ohio has contributed any distinctive literature to the nation, for it requires some striking physical characteristics or a peculiar population to bring out such forms of writing." That said, let it be noted Toledo was the home of Mildred "Millie" Wirt Benson, author of the original Nancy Drew mysteries.

Unlike Millie Benson, but like tens of thousands of other Toledoans in the years since the rust belt corroded, I left Toledo. I've lived on the East Coast for thirty-seven years. Yet I've never lost the sense of coming from the middle of nowhere. It's a good sense to have. Fifteen of those thirty-seven years were spent writing about politics in Washington, DC. Politicians, I've found, do not always know the difference between coming from nowhere and heading there.

People I've met in the East visit Toledo once in a while or, more often, pass through it. They remark on the featurelessness. They say, "It's so flat around there." A Toledoan would tell them, "So we can see you coming." I don't mind Easterners. But they think they're the best and brightest. In my opinion, Easterners have their best and brightest and we Toledoans have ours. Their best and brightest come up with things like FEMA, the budget deficit, and Iraq. Our best and brightest start a successful chain of muffler shops. From the best and brightest of the East Coast we get chaos and taxes. From the best and brightest of Toledo we get quiet cars.

A Toledoan would ask how, if people in the Midwest are so stupid, two midwestern companies—Arthur Andersen and Enron—managed to snooker almost every smart alec on both coasts. From a Toledo point of view, the important thing about New York is that New York is where the people from those strange, outlandish foreign countries come to first. They are required to stay there until they calm down and get enough common sense to move to Toledo. And the important thing about California is that every so often social, political, and economic forces cause a sort of tilt to occur in America. When America is tilted, everything loose rolls to California.

A Toledoan sees Toledo as a midwestern cornerstone, part of the foundation supporting the great edifice of the Midwest with its vital function of providing safety and sanity to the nation by keeping the East Coast and the West Coast apart. Toledoans do not want the hipsters of Berkeley and the stockbrokers of New York to become pals. Stocks in Toledo-based companies are doing badly enough without everyone going behind the Big Board to smoke goof butts. The last time that Wall Streeters got to know Californians, the result was the Silicon Valley dot.com tech bubble, and what few remaining pension plans and 401(k)s that Toledo had lost their pants.

And it is a terrifying idea that Hollywood and Washington, DC, might join forces for something more substantive than liberal fund-raising or

Arnold Schwarzenegger. The local multiplex could withhold the price of movie tickets and popcorn from paychecks each week. Movies would be four years long. And, if we don't get term limits, we'd have to see them again.

Toledo also helps keep the North and the South apart. Otherwise Minnesotans might be cutting eyeholes in their down comforters and burning symbols of secular humanism in the front yards of people who didn't contribute to NPR. And the chefs of Louisiana might season their gumbos with "Nebrasco" sauce.

A wonderful thing about Toledo is that it's a locality without local character—or characters. The supposed charms of folksy humor are mercifully absent. Toledo's old coots, unlike the old coots of Maine and Vermont, can give directions without telling you to turn left at the barn that burned down in 1954. Toledo has plenty of cows nearby, but Toledoans aren't fixated on cows the way Texas millionaires in their cowboy boots are. Toledo businessmen don't wear OshKosh overalls to the office. The parvenus of the New South build fake new *Gone with the Wind* houses. Toledoans don't. People from Ohio *won* the Civil War. We've still got our houses.

Toledoans don't often attempt to be inner-city, gangsta street-smart. We have Eminem to show us how midwesterners look doing that. And anyway, what kind of smart would that kind of Toledoan be? Ohio Turnpike smart?

Decorating fads do not come from Toledo. There is no Northwest Ohio equivalent of the "Southwest Style" that causes people in Seattle to build with adobe. Adobe is mud. It rains in Seattle. You won't see any *Martha Stewart Living* magazine spreads featuring Barcaloungers, TV trays, and Hummel figurines.

Toledoans love nature, but not in an unnatural way. No one from Toledo goes into the soybean fields to "become one with the manure." Protestors don't camp in the high corn during harvest season to "save the maize."

Teresa Brewer was from Toledo, proof that the city has no peculiar musical style with which to annoy the nation. Garage bands in Toledo stay in the garage.

Intellectual pretensions are held in check in Toledo. A Toledo boy does well at Libby High School. He ends up going to Harvard. On his first day he's walking across Harvard Yard and he asks an upperclassman, "Where's the library at?"

The upperclassman says, "Here at Harvard we don't end our sentences with a preposition."

"Okay," says the boy from Toledo, "where's the library at, asshole?"

Ideology does not stand the test of Toledo. Although Toledo is a resolutely proletarian city, Marxism never caught on. Imagine Toledoans reading *Das Kapital,* an entire huge book about the working class that never mentions bowling. And capitalism has not fared well either in Toledo, to judge by the number of big Toledo corporations—Autolite, Toledo Scale, Willys-Overland—that are gone from Toledo or just plain gone.

Deep thinking comes to pieces in Toledo. Freud is ridiculous—a man supposedly obsessed with sex but wholly ignorant of drive-in movies, Ottawa Park, and the back seats of cars. Existentialism is an epistemology of the here and now; and here I am now, in Toledo. The body paint and flower-decked tresses of the sixties were unsuited to Toledo's climate. As were sixties ideas. All you need is love (and galoshes). And feminism faced problems in Toledo. Gloria Steinem was born and raised here, yes, but it was Klinger in *M*A*S*H* who made the place famous.

I may be making Toledo sound dull, and it is. That's a godsend. Toledoans don't have to look long at the exciting events of history to realize how little those excitements contributed to human felicity. The humdrum is the source of decent pleasure. History would be a more cheerful story if history met the standards of "Toledo teen critique." When a teenager tells you, "There's nothing to do around here. Nothing ever happens," you know you're in the right historical time and place. (And you know that the proprietor of the hardware store is keeping a close eye on the spray paint and the inhalable solvents.)

Toledo is better than fun, it's happy. Perhaps it's the lack of deep thinking or distinctive literature. Nietzsche went crazy. Milton went blind. Danny Thomas and Jamie Farr went to Hollywood. Nothing is more conducive to sadness than taking yourself seriously. Every little lapse becomes a grave matter. Misplacing your bifocals is an international crisis if you think the whole world is depending on you to read life's fine print. You can't look at yourself in the mirror for shame (and for lack of bifocals). Taking yourself seriously is difficult when your baseball team is the Mud Hens.

Perhaps Toledo is happy because of the levelness. You need peaks to get valleys. There's not much envy among Toledoans. No matter how successful someone becomes, he's still from Toledo. And no land development pressures or geological barriers have kept Toledo from spreading out in that great leveling of lifestyles that snooty urbanites call suburban sprawl and that Toledoans call space for the aboveground pool.

Sprawl means time spent riding around in cars. Getting in a car always lifts the mood. Cars separate people from that principal source of depressive gloom, other people. (Unless you're packed in with the whole family on a days-long trip trying to find a mountain.) And economic stagnation has freed Toledo from traffic jams.

But mostly Toledo is happy because Toledoans are busy. People who live in places where there's nothing to do usually are busy. The Toledo area has thirty-eight public golf courses, and there are all those Dutch elm–diseased leaves to get out of the aboveground pool. It's in places that are overloaded with exotic diversions, like London, Paris, and New York, that people sit around doing nothing in restaurants, cafés, and coffee shops.

Toledo, from its very inception, seems to have been destined to avoid the fate of London, Paris, and New York. In 1836 Pierre Irving, nephew of Washington Irving, headed for what was then the frontier. Pierre intended to invest in land using a few thousand dollars entrusted to him by his uncle. En route Pierre wrote to a friend, "At the western extremity of Lake Erie . . . stands a town which some with a modest and inventive taste in names have called Toledo. It has an excellent harbour; is rapidly rising into importance, and in the opinion of many is [italics my own] *the germ of a second Buffalo.*"

I'd move back to Toledo if it weren't for my children. The world outside Toledo does not seem to be a happy or levelheaded place. And I want the kids to fit in.

about the author

PATRICK JAKE O'ROURKE was born in Toledo and grew up in the Jermain Park neighborhood. His father worked for the family Buick dealership on the East Side. His mother was the school secretary at Whittier Grade School. P. J. went to McKinley school, Devilbiss High (Class of '65), and Miami University (the real one—Miami was a university before Florida was a state). He is the author of eleven books, including *Holidays in Hell* (Atlantic Monthly Press, 1988), *Parliament of Whores* (Atlantic Monthly Press, 1991), *Eat the Rich* (Grove/Atlantic, 1998), and, most recently, *Peace Kills* (Atlantic Monthly Press, 2004). He writes for the *Weekly Standard* and lives in New Hampshire with his wife and three kids.

The Known to Which I Return

Alix Kates Shulman

CLEVELAND HEIGHTS

Alix Kates as a toddler in Cleveland, 1934

WHAT IS CLEVELAND TO ME? MIGHT AS
well ask what the earth and air are to me, for the spot of Cleveland
Heights where I grew up was my earth and air. As the very definition of
the real world, Cleveland was the unspoken standard by which the rest
of the world, glimpsed through books, stories, films, and hearsay, was
to be judged and interpreted. Until I was seventeen, Cleveland gave me
my eye and ear, my vocabulary and accent, my sense of Us and Them,
of Do and Don't, of Normal and Weird, of Familiar and Alien, of Home
and Beyond.

But no matter how devotedly I mastered the nuances of my hometown
mores, I could not help but discover the astonishing news that in some
places Cleveland pronunciation was considered an accent, that Cleveland
terminology was not universally comprehended, that Cleveland behav-
iors and rituals, dress codes and values were not everywhere acknowl-
edged. This dawning recognition came as such a shock as to catapult me
straight out into the larger world where I could investigate for myself
the fascinating and legendary differences of Elsewhere. But each discov-
ery of difference in my new and varying foreground—the wonders of
palm tree, cactus, ocean, mountain, fish knife, futon, featherbed—only
confirmed for me the solidity and uniqueness of my background: white,
suburban, middle-class Cleveland from childhood until the indelible
moment when I left in 1953.

My mother's sympathy, her scent, my father's guidance, his fedora, my
brother's summer ballgames on the radio, the vacant lots where we played
kick-the-can, the cinder path whose traces remain under the skin of my
knees, the endless variations of boys against girls, the club where Billie
Holiday sang, demanding Miss Edith Malen, who taught me to write in
an organized way, my immigrant grandparents' seders, the Public Library, the #32 Heights Express that whizzed us down Carnegie and Euclid to the Terminal Tower, barbecued ribs and pecan rolls—like a vivid
recurring dream, they remain in almost all my books as the given that is
questioned, the theme that is varied, the ground that is dug up, turned
over, and replanted, the known to which I endlessly return in order to
take my leave once more for the ever-beckoning and changing unknown.

The site of my dream was the single-family house on Ashurst Road
in Cleveland Heights, to which we moved from a rented side-by-side

when I was beginning kindergarten and my brother Bob first grade. Dad traded rent, which he considered wasteful, for equity, and Mom traded her indoor ferns for an outdoor garden, where each spring lilies of the valley, those delicate flowers scaled to a small child's hand, grew amid a border of blue myrtle. Over and over, I drew that house, from the age of four until I left it at twenty—first with pencil, then crayons, then charcoal, then watercolors—but I could never get to the bottom of it. It had a living-dining room, kitchen, lavatory, and tiny study on the first floor, three bedrooms and a bath on the second, and a slant-ceilinged room and bath with an old-fashioned claw-footed tub on the third. The long narrow living room, painted turquoise blue, held Mom's baby grand piano at one end and a folded drop-leaf table at the other. It would have been more efficient to keep the table always open instead of rolling it out each night at dinnertime, but Mom wanted the feeling of space. Bob's room was papered in a "masculine" brown-and-beige plaid, and my room—called the nursery, though my crib had gone directly to the third floor—in a pattern I selected: a blue-and-pink sky teeming with children swinging on stars and crescent moons. I was both stimulated and soothed as I lay in my grown-up bed studying the pattern's variations and repeats, filling my last waking moments with every combination of child, sky, star, and moon.

Outside, a sloping front lawn with two birch trees tall enough to enable me to earn the nickname "Climbing Kates" led to a three-step stoop. In picture after picture, Bob and I sit on the top step looking at the camera. Sometimes someone else is in the picture—our mother in a negligee with her arms around us, or one of our visiting aunts. But usually it's just us children. Here is Bob, seven or eight, slumped in a sunsuit, squinting glumly at the camera, while I sit beside him in a dark skirt and white blouse, knees spread in abandon like the tomboy I've become, head cocked inquisitively.

Once I launched my adolescence, the dream became disturbed. I was enthralled by story after story about leaving home to seek one's fortune, from *The Snow Queen* to *Rasselas* and *Candide*, to *Tristram Shandy* and *Don Quixote*. At night in my bed, when I was supposed to be asleep, I tuned my radio to New York City: jazz bands from Birdland and stories on *Grand Central Station* ("crossroads of a million private lives"). When my mother offered to have my room painted any color I liked, I chose a dark brown verging on black—yet another sign that Other and Elsewhere were calling me.

WHENEVER I RETURNED TO Cleveland after my move to New York, I clung to the difference between my new adult life and my encapsulated past. It was as if I needed to have nothing and no one ever change. I avoided driving through the old neighborhood, where our vacant lots had been obliterated by new houses and the new owners of our Ashurst house had painted it some dour inappropriate color. Once, after twenty years of living away, I returned to the Heights for a book signing to which all my high school friends were invited. That was in the early 1970s, when the country was in the throes of tremendous cultural upheaval. The smoldering social movements of the 1960s had burst into flame, we were at war in Vietnam, and I had become a passionate feminist, activist, and writer. Yet so little did those upheavals seem to have affected our suburb or my friends that I felt as if I were in a time warp.

Returning again more than a decade later for a thirty-fifth high school class reunion, I was amazed anew by how little had changed. More of my classmates than I'd ever have guessed were still married to their high school sweethearts or the catches they had famously landed in college before dropping out. Dick Levinsky was still a racetrack bum, Stan Grilli still grabbed the mike and sang, half the basketball team worked as managers or salesmen for their old team buddy, real estate mogul Herm Herman, cracking the same cynical sexist jokes. They danced the way we used to dance, the women cast critical eyes on one another's clothes, they met for lunch in the same old groups, were scandalized by the same stories. ("Why would you ever want to leave?" asked my friend Susan.)

It was true that by then everything that could happen to them had happened, just like elsewhere. They'd married, reproduced, traveled, divorced, remarried, started a business, made a bundle, gone bust, got elected to the board, resigned in disgrace, hit the bottle, kicked it, lost it all in Vegas, had passionate affairs, got caught in flagrante delicto, taken bribes, done coke, had facelifts, made a comeback, lost weight, gotten fat. They'd suffered with their addicted children and autistic grandchildren. They'd buried their mothers and survived their fathers-in-law.

They'd endured disappointment, indifference, ingratitude, mastectomies, hysterectomies, aneurysms, bypasses, transplants, implants, and every kind of cancer known to medicine. Yet their lives still seemed essentially unchanged. Even those who flew in from retirement condos in distant states might as well never have left (though Fran did take me aside to ask searchingly, "Tell me, how did you ever find the nerve to leave?").

I'D THOUGHT I'D NEVER return to Cleveland for longer than a weekend, never be comfortable there again. The Heights felt unreal to me, not life but a parody of life. But after my brother died, leaving to me the care of our elderly parents in their final years, and I began to immerse myself in the nitty-gritty of their affairs, the Heights gradually regained reality. Arriving at my parents' house from the airport soon began to feel as ordinary as returning home from work. My past and present were moving closer; if anything, it was my life elsewhere that sometimes seemed unreal.

Once my parents died—in 1996, seven months to the day apart—the wistful dream and quotidian reality merged. Writing my memoir *A Good Enough Daughter* about our lives together, from my earliest memories until their deaths, gave me a perspective I'd never had before, a perspective I needed for the task. With relief I found my life no longer bifurcated into a Here and Elsewhere, a Before and After, a Real and Other, but the singular whole every life must be—packed, varied, complete. And Cleveland finally assumed for me its proper place as neither idealized nor dreaded locus but as the historical, ineluctable site of my beginnings, my parents' lives, their parents' ends.

about the author

ALIX KATES SHULMAN's best-selling first novel, *Memoirs of an Ex-Prom Queen* (Knopf, 1972), has been called a "breakthrough book" for the feminist movement of the early 1970s. Shulman wrote three more novels, then a memoir, *Drinking the Rain* (Farrar, Straus and Giroux, 1995), about spending solitary summers on an island in Maine. Around that same time, she began returning to her native Cleveland to care for her aging parents, an experience she recounts in *A Good Enough Daughter* (Schocken, 1999).

Upon earning her BA, Shulman first left Cleveland for graduate school in New York City in 1953. After some years as an encyclopedia editor, she enrolled at New York University and, while raising two children, earned a degree in mathematics and later a master's degree in humanities. She became a feminist activist in 1967, published her first book in 1970 (*Bosley on the Number Line,* a children's book), and taught her first class in 1973—all lifelong pursuits that have found their way into her novels, nonfiction, and children's books. In 2000, she received an honorary doctorate from Case Western Reserve, her alma mater.

She still spends part of the year in Maine and the rest of her time in New York City with her partner of twenty years.

Small-Town Nice

It's not surprising that two writers, growing up hundreds of miles apart yet each in a small Ohio town of the 1950s and '60s, recall a culture of "niceness" pervading their childhoods. Dan Cryer in Findlay and Dale Keiger in Mt. Healthy both learned to respect friendly, polite, middle-class manners, like keeping your mouth shut if you don't have anything good to say. "Niceness, it was clear," Cryer writes, "embodied a bland, generalized condition of goodness that could be expanded infinitely in every direction."

Picture neighbors who wave hello to you each morning and know when to step in, with casseroles and compassion, because your mother is sick, as Cryer recalls. Picture streets and blocks and fields big enough to explore but not vast enough to lose yourself, as Jim Toedtman remembers about Berea. Such grounding, such security in knowing your place in the world, is why these writers cherish Ohio, no matter how far removed they are these days.

Literary journalist Ian Frazier has traveled the world, lived in the heart of Manhattan and on the western plains, and finally settled in New Jersey. But Frazier's hometown of Hudson remains his center of gravity, a measure by which he judges people and things.

"After growing up in Hudson, where anybody you met you already knew, you found it hard to take people from anyplace else quite seriously," Frazier writes. "They might be nice, and interesting, and all, but they had a transitory quality. Only people from Hudson who you'd known forever could be completely real."

Preacher's Kid

Dan Cryer

FINDLAY

Dan Cryer, second from right, the runt of his siblings

I WAS ONCE A PREACHER'S KID NAMED
Danny. This was not all bad. In fact, in the church-centered society that
was my hometown, it was distinctly a badge of honor.

Churches sprouted in Findlay like delis in New York City. There was
one on nearly every corner. In 1950, when I turned seven, there were
about forty-five churches serving a population of 23,845—one church
for every 530 people. My father, the Reverend Donald Cryer, presided
over 2,100-member First Methodist, an imposing Romanesque edifice
that eventually filled up an entire block near the center of town.

Churchgoing was part of Findlay's natural order, as inevitable as
going to school. As a boy, you attended Sunday school and Sunday serv-
ices, sang in the children's choir, thrilled to tales of Jacob's Ladder and
Noah's Ark at summer Vacation Bible School, joined the Boy Scouts for
knot-tying in the church basement, played second base on the church
softball team. Church, as much as school, was where you met your
friends and found a girlfriend. To be "unchurched" was rare, an admission that something had gone awry in your upbringing.

Ministers were respected community leaders who set the town's cultural and moral tone. Their sermons pointed the way to ethical living.
Their sage counsel eased strife among warring couples. Their prayers
blessed seniors at high school graduation ceremonies. From their ranks
leaders were tapped for the Elks, Odd Fellows, Masons, and Rotary
Club.

In the Findlay that I knew, being Christian meant being Protestant.
St. Michael's was the sole Catholic parish, never producing the critical
mass of students to require a parochial high school. So the few Catholic
kids in town attended Findlay High alongside young communicants
from First Methodist, First Presbyterian, Trinity Episcopal, First
Lutheran, Mason Chapel AME, Calvary Baptist, and all the rest. There
were only a handful of Jewish families in town and there was no synagogue. In my Bible-soaked mind, Jews were legendary Old Testament
characters rather than people living in the contemporary world. The
lone exception was Marlene Katz, my seventh-grade girlfriend, whose
family seems to have materialized out of nowhere and soon thereafter just
as quickly vanished.

Being a P.K. was mostly a blessing. It guaranteed me parents who loved me, pats on the head from kindly church ladies, and, in the grandest scheme of things, an inside track on salvation from sin.

Of course, this condition also ruled out a lot of excitement. Too many people were looking over your shoulder, ensuring that you followed the path of righteousness. So no one ever taught me to swear, smoke, or drink. Sex was forbidden premarital territory. No, I was too good for all that, too square, too white bread.

Any ventures into mischievousness never crossed the line into bad-boy misbehavior. I once skipped children's choir practice by crawling for an hour underneath the pews in the church sanctuary, hiding like a spy in enemy territory. I was a soldier, too, when very young. I would march around the kitchen, a pretend rifle on my shoulder, while singing "Onward, Christian Soldiers," thus confounding the evangelical with the martial.

Niceness was bred into me the way scions of the rich pick up a sense of entitlement about admission to the Ivy League. I was nurtured on it from birth. "If you can't say anything nice," the family mantra went, "don't say anything at all." Nice was simply the way people were, wasn't it? Certainly, the folks I encountered at church were. So it took many years to learn a basic truth: The world, which operated on less forgiving premises, wasn't designed to do me any favors.

The concept of "nice" covered a lot of ground. It wasn't reserved for good manners, a permanent smile, and an open, friendly nature. Calling a house "nice" meant that it was handsome, in a quiet neighborhood, and big enough to accommodate those ever-expanding fifties broods. A "nice" yard was tidy and well maintained. A "nice" car wasn't so much stylish as commodious and comfortable, certifying its owner's status squarely in the middle class. Niceness, it was clear, embodied a bland, generalized condition of goodness that could be expanded infinitely in every direction.

Methodists like me oozed nice. We wore Christianity's Good News on our faces. Anything but stuffy, we were smilers and touchers and back-patters. Affirming the egalitarian gospel of John Wesley, we reached out to each other, and the world, with an open-armed gusto.

And no wonder. Our theology promised hope rather than doom. Not fire and brimstone for us mainstream middle Americans, but a life of law-abiding decency and respectability in the here and now. We read the Bible not as literalists but as optimists. America offered more tangible rewards than any vague hereafter. Norman Vincent Peale's *Power of Positive Thinking*—linking self-esteem, good works, and worldly success— translated our everyday credo into a perennial best seller. (Peale was, after all, the son of a Methodist minister, a predecessor of my father's at First Church, Findlay, early in the century.)

Throughout my boyhood, niceness surrounded me like a womb, an ocean of tenderness. It was warm, all-embracing, and decidedly feminine. It sustained and nourished without making unreasonable demands, very much like a mother. When my own mother, Pauline Spitler Cryer, died at the age of forty-two in the fall of 1952, of complications from hypertension, when I was just eight, niceness took me into its arms and gave me shelter.

My mother's death was the central trauma of my boyhood, the gaping wound bandaged and swathed and partially healed by niceness, most notably in the form of my beloved grandmother. Grandma Cryer joined our household to soothe her grieving son and his four children with the selfless balm of her love. (Grandpa Cryer was another story, a sour grump of a failed farmer who sat by the radio for hours, listening to the Cleveland Indians claim a perpetual second place in the American League, except for the glory years of '48 and '54, to New York's Bronx Bombers.)

At First Methodist that year, other mothers and fathers showered me with caresses and kind words. Around our Christmas tree, set up two months after Mom's death, grew an enormous, ever-expanding mound of gifts from kindly parishioners—niceness even a kid could appreciate.

At Lincoln School, my fourth-grade teacher, a widow named Mary Garrison, was sensitive to my loss. Knowing that I loved to read history, when I was diagnosed in need of glasses, she showed me pictures of some of my heroes—Abe Lincoln, Benjamin Franklin, and so on—every one bespectacled. Now I, too, could join their distinguished company. A few years later she would become my stepmother.

My father was the oddest of half-breeds, the very embodiment of niceness yet a man quietly determined to claim a place of esteem in his provincial society. The cars he bought in mid-career said it all. Incapable of bargaining—how nice could that be?—he invariably paid sticker price for his Dodge, no questions asked. Even so, the color was usually red, an emblem of some decidedly un-Methodist, some flamboyant or hedonistic corner of his personality.

Bred on a farm not far from Findlay, Don Cryer took to the pulpit as though born to it. A gifted orator blessed with a mellifluous baritone, he quoted St. Paul and Shakespeare and the sentimental poetry of Edgar Guest. He memorized the names of every parishioner and knew whenever they were sick or had lost a job. To hoboes knocking on our back door for a handout, he was a soft touch. This was the same man who couldn't admit publicly his lofty heart's desire, always unrequited, to be elected a bishop of his church.

Here was our dirty little secret: Ambition was the flip side of the patented Cryer niceness. Consequently, our credo called for equal parts achievement and modesty. Excel in the classroom, on the playing field, and on the acting stage, but never brag about it. Be one of the quiet achievers, the guys who get the job done supremely well, without tooting your own horn. But for our niceness, our classmates would have loved to hate us. The sincerity of our smiles and goodwill provided armor against envy. They made our steady achievements seem altogether deserved.

"Always do your best," Dad reminded us with an athletic coach's single-mindedness. Embedded in this exhortation were several bits of wisdom. You were to work hard. You weren't supposed to cut corners, let alone cheat. You were to apply your God-given talents to the task and get things done. If you followed these guidelines and succeeded, that was terrific. If you failed, that was OK, too. You had done your best.

This achievement ethic governed every corner of life. When I entered the work world, as a paperboy for the *Toledo Blade*, I knew the morning news had to land on the customer's porch, not in a flowerbed. When I mowed Mrs. Purdy's lawn next door, I was never to miss a tell-tale strip of grass here and there. Keep the lawn tidy, I told myself, as if it were my own. (Only years later did I realize that this reclusive old woman—we kids regarded her as the neighborhood witch—was the mother of the celebrated novelist James Purdy.)

We Cryers weren't much good at revelry. We weren't drinkers or funny storytellers. Church socials and roller skating parties provided our low-key brand of fun. Just as our conversations skirted upsetting or controversial issues, we didn't have a clue about how to let our hair down. Without music, our lives might have been dismal. This was the open sesame unlocking an otherwise impenetrable vault of joy and passion. Some of us played in marching bands. My brothers formed combos that practiced in our living room, introducing me to the wonders of jazz. And all of us sang, raising a joyful noise in church and school choirs, appearing in one high school musical after another. We may have appreciated the Methodist hymnal, but we positively adored the Rodgers and Hammerstein songbook. Our annual Christmas card-newsletter was signed, "From the Cryer Choir."

In truth, for us, most forms of play amounted to work in disguise. The visceral pleasures of exercising or the exhilaration of winning often seemed secondary to the essential task of living up to your potential. Home alone on our driveway basketball court, I would hone my shooting skills for hours. When an opponent's hand was actually in my face, however, as a point guard for Lincoln Elementary, swishing those set shots wasn't nearly as easy. My potential, whatever it was, was proving to be frustratingly elusive.

Dad's pulpit oratory—always genial and warm, sometimes downright folksy—didn't shy away from sports talk. He would congratulate Ohio State's Buckeyes or Findlay's Trojans for a victory on the football field, commiserate in the face of defeat. For this small but muscled former gridder, taking note of athletic prowess came naturally. His two older sons, David and Jon, and a stepson, Bill Garrison, carried on the tradition.

Trailing behind these heroes of the gridiron, I was the runt of the litter. I was too small and too slow for the game. My football career peaked in sixth grade, when I was still able to compensate for a lack of size with determination and grit. By the time I reached junior high, I was pretending to be a quarterback, despite hands so tiny they could barely grip the ball. Humiliated, I quit the team in midseason.

Fortunately, I could match my older brothers in the classroom. It was unusual to bring home a report card with anything less than straight As. I recall one memorable slip—a C in math from that nice woman who became my stepmother—because I was delinquent in learning my multiplication tables. Other than another C—that math nemesis again—and a few stray Bs, the As ruled. It was much the same for my sister, Kathy Cryer, and stepsisters, Becky and Kay Garrison.

This record was the natural legacy of a household that revered the word. My father's home office-study testified to his commitment to learning. The shelves were laden with theology, history, biography, current events, and sermon collections. The Bible, of course, took pride of place. It was The Word, not because we kowtowed to every clause, but because it was western civilization's seminal book; it led the way to all other words. For me, it served not only as blueprint of divine order and ethical guide but also as treasure trove of stories. The cadences of the King James Version awakened me to the mesmerizing power of language. Here, within the confines of a single volume, lay the majesty of poetry, the wisdom of proverbs, the mystery of parables, the pageantry of the far away and long ago.

As I launched into a lifetime of reading, history's allure proved irresistible. The distance of time made Ohio's original residents, the Shawnee, Miami, and their neighbors, seem continents away. I loved to plunge into these other worlds, drowning my boyhood shyness in sheer otherness. What was it like, really, to track a deer with bow and arrow, to live in a "house" not made of sturdy brick?

At the public library, my boyhood hangout, I tended to curl up with biographies. Landmark Books for Young Readers, with their signature orange covers, allowed me to *Meet George Washington*, *Meet Betsy Ross*, *Meet Black Hawk* and other luminaries of American history. Without my realizing it, biography was becoming not only my gateway to history but the consummate link to Cryer ambition. I yearned to emulate my heroes. If I worked hard enough, followed my instincts, took some chances, pushed aside my fears, I, too, might succeed. I had no ambition to be president, let alone an Indian chief, but I was determined to find my path to success.

Was I channeling Norman Vincent Peale? No doubt, in some inchoate, juvenile fashion, I was.

The Power of Positive Thinking, according to *Publishers Weekly,* was the number 6 best-selling book in the year of its publication, 1952, and it remained triumphant in the nonfiction top 10 through 1955. If its impact on the nation was enormous, on our family it was incalculable. To my father, Peale was a beacon of hope, an inspiring rebuttal to intellectual doomsayers mired in alienation and despair. While sophisticates scorned Peale's message as simplistic salesmanship dressed up in Christian doctrine, Don Cryer defended him as "the most maligned man in America."

Peale announced the book's essential message, and its unmistakable tone, in his opening lines: "Believe in yourself! Have faith in your abilities!" This pioneer of self-help approached the genre in unabashedly Christian terms. You ought to believe in yourself, he suggested, because God believed in you. Homely anecdotes about businessmen who overcame self-doubt and climbed the company ladder were buttressed by one confidence-boosting Bible verse after another. "I can do all things in Christ which strengtheneth me," Paul's Letter to the Philippians counseled.

"Whatever you're doing, give it all you've got. . . . Hold nothing back," Peale echoed and updated. "Keep the idea of prosperity, and of attainment firmly fixed in your mind. Never entertain a failure thought. . . . Affirm aloud, 'God is now giving me success.' . . . Visualize achievement."

It was easy to sneer at what seemed like vapid optimism. In place of Peale's upbeat go-getters, realists could point to Arthur Miller's battered, defeated salesman, launched into the world three years earlier, as the more typical Everyman. However sound their judgments, critics tended to overlook that this New York City–based pastor was a farsighted champion of modern psychology and psychiatry. Whatever he was, he was no rube. The debate, in any case, took place well outside my boyish purview. I was too busy imbibing Peale's maxims at my father's knee.

Peale knew from experience, he noted in an aside, that "preacher's sons are supposed to be nice and namby-pamby." Any true reckoning of my boyhood must take into account that observation's partial truth. Yes, we Cryers were nice as can be. But no one would have described us as "namby-pamby." We were fighters. We were winners.

In the middle of my sophomore year of high school, my father was transferred to a church in Middletown, 135 miles to the south. However stressful, this uprooting proved to be a marvelous chance to start over. I no longer had to follow in the footsteps of three superachiever brothers. I was my own man in the making. At Middletown High, I flourished as never before—as honor student, student council vice president, award-winning orator, versatile character actor, varsity tennis player, even feisty intramural basketball and touch football player. Armed with equal parts ambition and "niceness," I was well on the road to making it. This was the Ohio-bred ethos that would shape whatever intelligence and talent this preacher's kid had been given.

What followed was no unbroken victory parade into manhood. There were plenty of false starts and downright failures ahead. One brute fact blocked the way forward: My mother Pauline was gone. Hence the war raging forever inside my head, Peale's cheerleading gamely battling the relentless yammer of negativity. No one had to inform me that bad things happen to good people.

In the end, niceness proved ineffectual in the face of overwhelming grief. My coping strategy was repression. All memories of Pauline, this gentle daughter of a country doctor, faded away. Deprived of her, the hurt paradoxically diminished. Still, she would remain hidden away somewhere in my gouged-out heart—adored, yearned for, fitfully imagined, ultimately unknowable.

about the author

DAN CRYER served as book critic at *Newsday* for twenty-five years. He has been a finalist for the Pulitzer Prize in criticism and vice president of the National Book Critics Circle. His book reviews have appeared in the *New Republic*, the *Washington Post*, *Salon*, the *Boston Globe*, the *Chicago Tribune*, the *Christian Science Monitor*, the *San Francisco Chronicle*, the *Plain Dealer*, and other publications. Cryer contributed to *The Salon.com Reader's Guide to Contemporary Authors* (Penguin, 2000), *Conversations with William Kennedy* (University

Press of Mississippi, 1997), and *Conversations with Louise Erdrich and Michael Dorris* (University Press of Mississippi, 1994). He is a graduate of the College of Wooster and earned a PhD in U.S. history at the University of Minnesota. He and his wife live in New York City.

Out of Ohio

Ian Frazier

HUDSON

Main Street, Hudson, looking north, 1968 (courtesy Hudson Library and Historical Society)

RECENTLY I SAW IN A NEWSPAPER

from Hudson, Ohio, my hometown, that they were about to tear down the town's water tower. In principle, I don't care anymore how things I used to love about Hudson change or disappear. Each time a big change happens, though, I feel a moment of resistance before my lack of caring returns. The town's water tower, built in the early nineteen hundreds, was its civic reference point, as its several white church steeples were its spiritual ones. The water tower was higher than they, and whenever you were walking in the fields—the town was surrounded by fields—you could scan the horizon for the water tower just above the tree line and know where you were. The cone-shaped top, and the cylindrical tank below it, gave the water tower the aspect of an old-time spaceship, though more squat. Its dull silver color and the prominent rivets in its sheet-metal side added to the antique Buck Rogers look. Or, to switch movies, the tower looked like the Tin Man in *The Wizard of Oz*. Two generations ago, water towers like this one could be found superintending small towns all over the Midwest and West. I'm sure the Tin Man was even based on them.

I lived in Hudson from when I was six until I was eighteen. Sometimes I try, usually without success, to describe how sweet it was to grow up in a small Ohio town forty years ago. As I get into the details, corniness tinges my voice, and a proprietary sentimentality that puts people off. I say the names of my friends from back then—Kent, Jimmy (called Dog), Susie, Bitsy, Kathy, Charlie (called Dunkie), Timmy, Paul—and they sound somehow wrong. They're like the names of characters in nostalgic mid-American movies or Bruce Springsteen songs, and I start to think of us as that myself, and a blurring sameness sets in, and the whole business defeats me. But then a friend from Hudson calls, or I run into somebody from there, or I hear the rattle of shopping-cart wheels in a supermarket parking lot, and for a second I remember how growing up in Hudson could be completely, even unfairly, sweet.

Most modern people don't belong to any place as intimately as we belonged to Hudson. Now the town has grown and merged with northern Ohio exurbia, so it's hardly recognizable for what it was. Some of the old sense of belonging, though, remains. A while ago, I went back for a funeral. I took the bus from New York City to Cleveland overnight and then drove down to Hudson in the morning with my brother. We walked into Christ Church, our old church, now unfamiliar because of remodeling, and sat in the back. I saw not many people I knew. Then, over my shoulder, in the aisle, I heard a woman say, "I think I'll just sit here next to Sandy Frazier."

To return home, to have a person call me by name; and to look up and remember her, forty-some years ago, as a junior-high girl in Bermuda shorts at the town's Ice Cream Social, an event sponsored by the League of Women Voters on the town green, where I and my friends chased her and her friends between tables and chairs and across the lawn flicking wadded-up pieces of paper cups at them with long-handled plastic ice-cream spoons, bouncing the missiles satisfyingly off the girls as they laughed and dodged—

I should finish that thought, and that sentence. But the service had begun for Cynthia, a friend to my family and me. She was dead at sixty-seven of Lou Gehrig's disease. Back in the nineteen sixties, someone climbed the water tower and wrote Cynthia's name on it, billboard-large, a declaration of love. It stayed there above the trees for a long time, until the town painted it over. When I was eight or nine, Cynthia made a point of coming up and saying hello to me in the basement of the Congregational church. I was there, I think, because my mother was helping with the scenery for a play. When I was just out of high school, Cynthia heard me telling my friends a story in her living room, and afterward she told me I would be a writer. When I was in my twenties, I came back to town one night from hitchhiking someplace east or west, and I found nobody home at our house, so I went over to Cynthia's, and she put on a bathrobe and came downstairs and heated up a bowl of soup for me and sat with me at the island in the middle of her kitchen as I ate.

In those days I was constantly leaving town. Hudson was made for leaving. The Ohio turnpike, also called Interstate 80, crossed the town from east to west behind a chain-link fence. The distant sound of traffic on the turnpike was part of the aural background of the town, like the rising and falling of the whistle in the Town Hall every noon. After the turnpike, other interstates came nearby. In Hudson Township, you could go from shady gravel road to two-lane county asphalt to far-horizon, four-lane interstate highway in just a few turns of the steering wheel.

When I left the first time to go to college—the original leaving, which set a pattern for later ones—my plane to Boston was on a Sunday morning, and I spent all the preceding day and night going around town, seeing friends, saying good-bye, standing and talking under streetlights in hushed, excited tones. Early Sunday, I was lying on the floor of a living room with Kent, Bitsy, and Kathy, listening over and over to the song "Leaving on a Jet Plane." Nobody was saying anything. The girls were quietly crying, not so much about my leaving as about the overwhelmingness of everything; the year was 1969. I cried, and also pretended to cry, myself. From ground level I looked at the nap of the rug and the unswept-up miscellany under the couch. I would never be even a tenth as at home anywhere again.

Four years later, I graduated with a degree in General Studies and no clear plans. Mostly I wanted to go back home. I had had enough of the East, a place I was unable to make much sense of. My college girlfriend, Sarah, whom I was too self-absorbed to be able to appreciate, became fed up with my increasingly wistful hometown reminiscences as graduation day approached. "Don't invite me to your Ohio wedding" was one of her last remarks to me. After I received my diploma, my father came over to me in the courtyard of my dorm as I was talking to friends and hugged me so hard he lifted me off the ground. We loaded the trunk of the family Maverick with my belongings, the textbooks dumped in any which way, and drove straight home on Interstate 90 and the turnpike, arriving before dawn. I stayed awake and had some scrambled eggs my mother made, and then I went into the yard and watched the sunrise through the newly leafed trees. It rains a lot in northeastern Ohio, so the trees are extremely green. All around me, the summer landscape draped like a big hammock. I felt geographically well situated, and defiantly at home.

I didn't bother to take my books out of the trunk of the car—just left them in there, rattling—and a few days later someone ran into my mother from behind on Middleton Road, and they scattered everywhere and got run over. My mother, as of course she would, carefully retrieved them. I still have several of them—for example, *The Power Elite,* by C. Wright Mills, with a black Ohio tire tread running across the cover.

Why did Hudson enchant me? Why was life, there and then, so sweet? I think a million reasons happened to come together, none of which we grasped at the time. We had plenty of leisure. We had cars to drive. Gasoline was so cheap it was practically free. Our parents, to whom the cars we drove belonged, had leisure, too. In their ease, they were inclined to take long vacations, and indulge us kids. Fathers (and a few mothers) had steady jobs, pensions, and health insurance. The economic difficulties that would later take a lot of those away and that I still don't understand had not yet visibly begun. Vietnam was winding down. The draft had just ended, removing a load from all our minds. Et cetera.

In my case, life was good, by comparison, because it had recently been so bad. The previous December, my fifteen-year-old brother, Fritz, had died of leukemia. After that, the last thing my parents wanted to do was to keep my other siblings and me from having any fun we could have. Dad and mom would be gone a lot of that summer, traveling in India. At our house, I would be in charge.

And then, as a further reason for life's sweetness, there was hot, drowsy, hilly, expansive Ohio itself. Not so many people lived in Ohio then, and its commercial sprawl had narrower limits. Some of the local roads were still dirt and bisected working farms. Everybody still knew everybody. At Kepner's Bar on Main Street, I might run into a woman in a wild dress and hoop earrings who, as it turned out, I'd known since first grade. To the west of town, on the turnpike, the highway went through a cut topped with a scenic (though otherwise unnecessary) bridge supported by a graceful arch that framed a mega-screen view of the Cuyahoga River Valley and sunlit points beyond. Too big to punish, we could now go where we wanted; a kid I knew got the urge to hitchhike to the East Coast one afternoon and set out in his bare feet and traveled barefoot the whole journey. I was done with school—finally and thoroughly done. Vague possibilities shimmered in every direction.

Back then it seemed there was a lot more room, especially outdoors. In a town like Hudson every piece of ground did not have to account for itself in real-estate terms, as it does today. On the edges of town and sometimes beside roads and buildings were plots of weedy, dusty, driven-over earth that no one had given much thought to since Hudson began. At the Academy, where I went to high school, the shadows of trees at sunset stretched three hundred yards across the school's lawns. Often on summer evenings we played Wiffle ball there. The game was like baseball, only with a plastic ball that didn't go as fast and wobbled in flight, and could be caught barehanded. You didn't need shoes, either, in the lawn's soft grass.

After a game of Wiffle ball at sunset—after running enormously far across the lawn to catch foul balls, sliding shirtless into base on close plays, reclining itchily in the grass waiting to bat, quitting the game only when it was too dark to see the ball—we would go to the beverage store downtown and stand in the pleasantly frigid walk-in cooler, deciding whether to buy the evening's supply of Stroh's beer by the twelve-pack or the case. And then the evening would continue. At this hour, girls we knew would be sitting on somebody's front porch smoking cigarettes. Twenty minutes of driving around would discover them.

That summer, a woman I'd gone out with when she was a girl happened to be in town. Her family had moved to Wheaton, Illinois, but she had come back to stay with her sister, who lived in an apartment above a store on Main Street. I climbed the outdoor stairs and knocked on the apartment door, and Susie came out, keeping one ear open for her sleeping nephew, whom she was babysitting. We were kissing at the bottom of the stairs in the shadows when she considered me for a moment and declared, "You're a real person."

The "you" was emphasized: "*You're* a real person." She meant this not as a compliment but as a statement of fact. I understood what she meant. After growing up in Hudson, where anybody you met you already knew, you found it hard to take people from anyplace else quite seriously. They might be nice, and interesting, and all, but they had a true transitory quality. Only people from Hudson you'd known forever could be completely real.

Now I see Hudson as the place where I was spun and spun throughout my childhood in order to have maximum velocity when it finally let me go. My leaving-for-good happened like this:

I hung around that summer until my presence became otiose. Friends' parents started asking me how long I would be in town. My parents, back from India, began to suggest chores, like mowing the lawn. There's a certain nightmare time-warp feeling that can come over you—a sense that you're your present size but sitting in your old desk from elementary school, with your knees sticking up on the sides. The feeling can motivate you to plunge into any uncertainty, just so long as it's present tense. One morning in late August I packed a suitcase, jumped the turnpike fence, and began to hitchhike west.

First, I went to visit my best friend and former neighbor, Don, in Colchester, Illinois. Colchester is smaller than Hudson and more intoxicatingly Midwestern. The backyards on Don's street were all clotheslines and garden rows of corn, and beyond the corn ran the tracks of a main rail line bound for St. Louis. Don and his friends and I used to smoke dope and sit by the tracks at night waiting for the eleven-o'clock train. At first it was a little, faraway light, and then suddenly it grew into a blaring, blue-white beam and gigantic noise pounding immediately by. Then in a while the night would be its quiet self again. Just to lie in the back bedroom of Don's house with the curtains billowing inward on the breeze was middle-of-the-country nirvana for me.

From Colchester I continued on to Chicago, where I got a job on a European-style skin magazine published by *Playboy*. The magazine's editor had written to the *Harvard Lampoon*, which I had worked for in college, and had offered a job to any *Lampoon* person who wanted one. The offices were cave-like, with halls resembling tunnels and fragrant darkbrown corkboard paneling on the walls. In a short while, I learned that writing captions for photos of naked women is a particular talent, one that is surprisingly difficult to fake. I quit the day I was supposed to get a company ID card, which I feared would be a raised bunny head—the *Playboy* logo—stamped on a photo of my face.

Then I lay around my small North Side apartment for a few months on the bare mattress that was its only furniture and read books or looked at the plaster floret on the ceiling. Somewhere I had come across Hemingway's list of the novels he thought it essential for every writer to know and I started in on them. I also spent weeks at a time in uninterrupted, not uncomfortable despair. On Wednesdays, I would go to the newsstand across from the Ambassador East Hotel and buy the latest issue of the *New Yorker*, and then on my mattress I would read every word in it, including the columns of small type in the front. When Pauline Kael reviewed a movie by Sam Peckinpah, I told Susie that Kael had called him "a great and savage artist," and that I wanted people someday to say the same about me. Susie was going to school at the University of Northern Iowa at Cedar Falls. I sometimes took long Greyhound bus rides out to visit her.

My grandmother, a can-do person who enjoyed the challenge of setting wayward relatives on their feet, sent me many letters telling me to come visit her in Florida, and after about the fourth letter I agreed. Before I left Chicago, I gave up my apartment. The landlord was glad to get rid of me. He said that he thought my mattress, surrounded as it was by all the books and magazines I'd been reading, constituted a fire hazard. From Chicago I rode Greyhound buses for forty-five hours to Key West. On one bus I saw a skinny white guy with combed-high hair try to pick up a black woman sitting next to him, and when she politely moved to another seat he drank a pint or two of whiskey, began to shout at his reflection in the bus window, asked the old woman in front of him if she was wearing a wig, pulled her hair to find out, and eventually left the bus in handcuffs under the escort of the highway patrol, an expression of calm inevitability on his face. Between Georgia and Miami, I listened through the night to a Vietnam veteran with hair longer than Joni Mitchell's talk about a Vietnamese woman he had killed during the war, and about many other topics, his words flowing unstoppably and pathologically until I almost came to hate him. When I finally shot him an angry look, he gave me back a stare of such woefulness and misery that I was ashamed. Out of South Miami I sat next to a psychiatrist who explained to me in psychological terms why the passengers sitting near him objected to his chain-smoking. He was the only seatmate I openly argued with. When my grandmother met me at the Key West bus station, I was furious at her for all I'd been through.

Unlike my parents, Grandmother did not believe in depression. If my mother fell into a gloom, she usually nurtured it into a dark and stationary front that hung over the kitchen for days. As for my father, his strategy when he became depressed was to move from a regular level of depression as much further down the scale as he could possibly go, getting more and more depressed and thinking up consequent sorrows and disasters of every kind until he reached a near panic state. Then when he came to himself again, and looked at the actual situation, it seemed not so terrible after all. Grandmother's approach, by contrast, was never to give depression that smallest advantage. Whenever she sensed its approach, she attacked it and routed it and slammed the door.

In Key West, she didn't even allow me to be horizontal for longer than eight hours of sleeping a night. Early in the mornings, she appeared at the front desk of the Southern Cross Hotel, where she had rented me a small room, and she sent the plump and sarcastic German manager to pound on my door with a German-accented witticism. Then she would give me breakfast and hurry me off to the job she had found for me, doing gardening work for a lady even older than she, Minona Seagrove. Minona Seagrove walked very slowly and couldn't really bend down, but she loved to garden, and every day I served as her robot gardening arms, trimming palmetto fronds and planting bulbs while she stood behind me and said what to do. In the evenings, Grandmother made dinner for me and my cousin Libby, who was also visiting. Then sometimes we would play long games of Scrabble with Grandmother, her friend Marjorie Houck, and a very old English lady named Mavis Strange, who consistently won, using words that are in the dictionary but nobody has heard of.

Grandmother's closest friend, Betty Stock, had a daughter named Isabel who worked for the *New Yorker*. Under the name Andy Logan, Isabel wrote the Around City Hall column for the magazine. Just before graduation, I had halfheartedly applied to the *New Yorker* for a staff-writing job. Grandmother said if I tried again she would ask Betty to ask Isabel to put in a word with the editor for me. This idea seemed kind of farfetched, but I said OK: I hadn't brooked Grandmother in anything so far. Grandmother didn't like my hair, so she sent me to her longtime hairdresser and had him cut it. It came out looking bad, though not as bad as I had expected. Grandmother also went through my wardrobe, if it could be called a wardrobe, and singled out a pair of khaki slacks, a shirt, and a blue sweater as acceptable clothing to wear for New York job interviews. I trusted her unquestioningly as an authority on what well-dressed office workers in New York City wore.

After a month or so of this retooling, Grandmother was satisfied and ready for me to move on. Libby drove me in Grandmother's Ford Fairlane a few miles up the Keys to a good place to hitchhike. In a night-and-day hitchhiking marathon, I made it from the Keys to Morgantown, Kentucky, where my friend Kent was doing volunteer work for the Glenmary Home Missioners. Along the way, I got some wacky Southern rides, including one across South Carolina with a Post Office driver in a small refrigerated truck carrying, he said, "human eyeballs." He was taking them to an eye bank somewhere.

In late afternoon, I arrived at the slant-floored mountain shack Kent had rented, and I was so tired that I immediately lay down and fell asleep on a bed in a side room. It happened that Kent was having a party for the entire community that night. As the guests came in, they piled their coats on top of the bed, on top of me. At the party's height a man and a woman entered the room and closed the door and, not knowing I was there, lay down on the coats and began to talk about the extramarital affair they were having. I emerged from sleep to the sound of their French-movie-type dialogue: "Oh, Roger, I've felt like crying for the last three days!" "Oh, Arliss, [mumble mumble mumble]." Then suddenly the door opened, and from it, like a super-loud PA system, the voice of the outraged husband: "Get out of that fuckin' bed, Roger!" The two men adjourned outside for a fistfight while the woman stayed on the coats, sobbing. I began to stir, poking part of my head out from under. The sobbing stopped; silence; then, in complete bafflement, "Who's *he*?"

A few days later I was back in Hudson. At this slow time of year, none of my friends were around, except Kathy. She had a job at a small, classy store on Main Street that sold women's clothes. I thought that now would be a good opportunity to tell her of the crush I had on her, but as I stood in the store watching her refold sweaters or sat with her on the couch in her family's TV room talking about what our other friends were doing, the moment never came up. Late one night, I went over to her house with an idea of throwing some pebbles at her window, waking her, and telling her how I felt. When I approached through the backyards, the light was still on in her bedroom; as I got closer I saw in the dimness a guy at the edge of her lawn staring so raptly at her window that he never noticed me.

I faded back into the next yard and cut across it and then went to the sidewalk, and as I passed by the front of Kathy's house I saw a cigarette glow on the front steps. She was sitting there, and didn't seem at all surprised to see me. I told her about the guy in her backyard and she smiled. She had a quick smile that went horizontally, like a rubber band stretched between two fingers. The corners of it were so cute they drew your eyes into close-up frame. With undisguisable happiness she said, "That was John."

And so on to New York City. Early one morning before work, Kathy gave me a ride to exit 13 on the turnpike, just east of town. Local hitchhiking wisdom said that more eastbound trucks got on the highway there. After a friendly hug across the front seat I got out and she drove away. I carried my same suitcase and a cardboard sign on which I'd written "NYC" in large letters with a Magic Marker. I was keyed up. I hadn't asked my parents for money—some of my Minona Seagrove earnings still remained—and I intended not to come back without something to show. I stood, heroic to myself, on the shoulder of the on-ramp in the smell of diesel and the gusts from traffic blowing by. After half an hour or so, a truck pulled over. That moment is always a thrill, when the air brakes hiss and the big machine swerves over and stops just for you. I ran to it, threw my suitcase up through the open door, and climbed the rungs to the cab.

I didn't go very far that day. Many short rides and long waits put me after nightfall at a truck stop in central Pennsylvania. The place had a dormitory floor upstairs with a dozen beds for truckers and bathrooms with showers. I signed the register in my own name, boldly wrote down that I drove for Carolina Freight, and paid my five dollars for a narrow metal-frame bed. I slept well in a room with a changing group of truckers, each of whom put in his few sleeping hours determinedly and then was gone. In the morning I showered, ate a big breakfast in the restaurant, and, caffeinated and pleased with the day so far, stood by the parking-lot exit sign with my sign.

The truck that pulled over for me there looked so unpromising that I hesitated before getting in. The tractor was gas-powered, not diesel, with a rusty white cab and a small trailer—the kind of rig, smaller than an eighteen-wheeler, that hauls carnival rides. Its driver appeared equally off-brand. He had strands of black hair around his too-white face and he lacked a few teeth. After saying hello, he told me that he had just taken a lot of methamphetamines. I asked if he was feeling them yet, and he whipped off his sunglasses and said, "Look at my eyes!" Bedspring spirals of energy seemed to be radiating from his black irises. He was beating on the steering wheel with his palms, fiddling with the all-static radio, and moving from one conversational topic to another randomly.

It is perhaps unfair to say that drivers of carnival trucks are horny guys; free-floating lust howls down every highway in the world, sweeping all kinds of people along. This particular speed-popping driver, however, closely fit the horny-guy profile. As his conversation caromed around, it kept returning to, and finally settled on, the subject of a whorehouse he said was not far up the road. He talked about how much he liked it, and what he did there, and the girls who worked in it, and the old man who owned it, and how popular he, the driver, was there.

Soon the driver was going to suggest that he and I make a visit to this whorehouse. I could tell; clearly his drift tended no other way. As he went on, I considered how I would respond. Sanity said, obviously, no. Under no circumstances go to a whorehouse with this guy. Say thanks but no thanks, and jump out as soon as possible. I was ready to be sane and do that. But then I thought . . . I wasn't bound for New York just to demur and make my apologies. Begging off anything at this point didn't feel right. New York City was the big time, and I wanted to be big-time when I got there. When the moment came to jump, I intended to jump. Right then the guy turned to me with a wicked and challenging glint to his sunglasses. Almost before the words left his mouth I thanked him politely and said that yes, going to this whorehouse sounded like an excellent idea.

For a while after that, the guy fell silent. I flattered myself that maybe I'd taken him by surprise. He turned the truck off the highway and proceeded along a two-lane country road. I had no idea what I would do when we got to the whorehouse. The thought of going to it scared me dizzy. I figured I would come up with a plan when I had to. Ahead I saw a tall, narrow, three-story house, its barred windows sealed inside with blinds. A small neon beer sign lit a side door. "There she is!" the driver said, perking up. No cars were in the gravel parking lot as he coasted in, downshifting. He leaned across the dash and pulled over by the side door to examine it closely, giving a few light taps on the horn. No reply or sign of life. More taps on the horn. A few minutes passed. Then, reluctantly, he concluded that no one was about, and he headed back to the highway.

Oh, the intense and private joy of the uncalled bluff! Until now I had experienced it only in games. This felt a hundred times greater than any game. Keeping my face nonchalant I exulted inwardly, and made a resolve that in my life in New York City I would bluff whenever the occasion arose. At that moment on the road in the middle of Pennsylvania, I quit living in Hudson and began to live in the world.

The guy left me off someplace in eastern Pennsylvania. By then, the pills he had taken had evidently set him back down, and he looked different, kind of shriveled and mumbly, behind the wheel. I was relieved to be shut of him and out of his spooky cab, and I shouted with the pleasure of being alone as soon as his truck was out of sight. The next ride I got was with a guy about my age from San Isidro, Costa Rica. He must've been part Indian, because he had straight black hair like a Sioux's and an Aztec nose. He was littler than a Sioux, though, and olive skinned. He drove a big-engine car, the kind they had back then that looked like slabs, and its rear seat was full of cardboard boxes of his stuff. He had lived in Chicago and was moving to New York City, he said. I told him I was, too. With a companion we knew better each of us might have been cooler and more restrained, but as he maneuvered the big car through Jersey traffic we cheered at the first glimpse of the city skyline faintly gray on the horizon.

I hadn't seen a lot of cities then, and I didn't know that New York, to a traveler coming from the west, affords the best first-time, big-city view in the U.S.A. The guy from Costa Rica and I cruised across the long and splendid drum roll of open-sky swamp up to the Hudson River. Then we swerved down the elevated highway toward the Lincoln Tunnel, and the city suddenly and manifestly filled the windshield and side windows, rising from the Hudson as if lifted by eyelids when you opened your eyes. No skyline I know of is its equal; across the windows it ran, left to right, like a long and precise and detailed and emphatic sentence ending with the double exclamation points of the World Trade Center towers.

It was a mild day in early March, just before rush hour. Lights had come on in some of the buildings, and dusk was beginning to gather in the spaces between them. We went through the Lincoln Tunnel and popped up on the city floor, with buildings and vehicles impending all around. Our windows were open; the city smelled like coffee, bus exhaust, and fingernail polish. The Costa Rican was going to stay with relatives in Queens, a place as exotic to me then as Costa Rica. I was going to Greenwich Village to meet my friend David, who had told me he could find me a place to stay. I got out at Thirty-fourth and Seventh, the southwest corner. When I pass by that corner occasionally today, I still think of it as the place where I landed. The Costa Rican and I wished each other good luck, without pretending to exchange phone numbers (we didn't have them, anyway) or saying we'd keep in touch. We were now a little part of the other's past, and in New York the past was gone.

about the author

As a humorist, literary journalist, and essayist, Ian Frazier often combines first-person narrative with in-depth reporting. His books, such as *Great Plains* (Farrar, Straus and Giroux, 1989) and *On the Rez* (Farrar, Straus and Giroux, 2000) look closely at Native Americans, fishing, and the outdoors. Other books, like *Dating Your Mom* (Farrar, Straus and Giroux, 1986) and *Coyote v. Acme* (Farrar, Straus and Giroux, 1996), poke fun at modern culture with an intelligent, creative wit. With *Family*, Frazier traces the stories of his relatives from his great-grandparents to his siblings and their Hudson, Ohio, upbringing. His latest book is a collection of essays on place, *Gone to New York: Adventures in the City* (Farrar, Straus and Giroux, 2005).

Frazier attended Harvard University, where he was on the staff of the *Harvard Lampoon.* Several years later he joined the staff of the *New Yorker*, where he wrote feature articles, humorous sketches, and pieces for the Talk of the Town section. He continues to write for the *New Yorker* as well as the *Atlantic Monthly, Outside,* and other publications. Frazier lives in Montclair, New Jersey, with his wife, author Jacqueline Carey.

Two Towns, Arguing

Dale Keiger

MT. HEALTHY, ATHENS

Dale Keiger

AN UNUSUAL RUN OF WARM DECEMBER
weather lets me linger after dinner on a street corner in Athens, Ohio.
Athens is a college town. Every September the students of Ohio University double its population, fill its coffers, and disturb its equilibrium. In the early 1970s, I was one of them. Now I live near Baltimore, but I visit Athens a few times every year and become a solitary, contented wanderer, sauntering down its sidewalks and brick paths immersed in a rich suspension of past and present. In this building I sat for my first college class, Psych 101. In this house, which used to be yellow, I was sick from an ill-advised intake of beer and cheap wine. Here is the coin laundry on State Street where I washed my clothes at 3:00 a.m. and read Carlos Castaneda. And here is Read Hall, where late one night in the mud of its commons I wrestled with three other guys while my future girlfriend, whom I had not yet met, gazed down from a dormitory window and thought, *Look at those idiots.*

Now, thirty years on, I pause and gaze across the street to a balcony above a sandwich shop. Paint peels from its white railing and it looks none too substantial. On another warm night, in 1975, I sat on that balcony and smoked a joint with the production manager of the university's student newspaper. That I so casually violated the drug laws was not unusual for the time or place, but represented a profound change in me. In 1972 I left my hometown for college as a scrawny hick from a small town near Cincinnati with no experience of the world, no ambition, and little understanding of myself. I left four years later urgent to become a novelist, with at least the beginnings of self-knowledge and the first green shoots of a literary sensibility. Today, when I read something I've written, I hear one set of formative experiences grafted to the rootstock of another. I hear two Ohio towns.

The one I was raised in bears the too-good-yet-true name of Mt. Healthy, 1.4 square miles in area and population 7,149 as of the last census. It sits about twenty miles northwest of Cincinnati, so it's not exactly a rural hamlet, but in those days the police force numbered three, the high school's homecoming parade went down the main street every autumn, and there was an actual village idiot, a hapless soul named Albert. It was populated mostly by conservative, pragmatic, and unimaginative white folk, the working-class descendants of Germans and Ulster

Scots, born in Ohio and with no plans to go anywhere else as long as they had jobs. On my street were a cop, a postal worker, a used-car salesman, a lineman for Cincinnati Gas and Electric, a mill worker, a factory worker, and a sign painter. The sign painter was my dad.

Until it was renamed to commemorate having been a refuge from the cholera epidemic of 1850, Mt. Healthy was called Mt. Pleasant, and I was raised to be pleasant. We all were. Mention the Midwest to people who are not from there and you may hear in response, "Isn't that where everybody's nice?" The degree of wryness, bemusement, or condescension will vary person to person, but the observation isn't off by much. Midwestern parents of the 1950s and 1960s raised my generation to be polite, to be modest, and to avoid anything that might provoke. I remember listening to a radio report on a man in Iowa who had lost his house, his possessions, and his farm to a massive flood. When the reporter thanked him for his time, he replied, "You're welcome, ma'am, and you have a nice day now." That, to me, was purebred midwestern. A churning, rain-swollen river had just washed away this man's life. But he'd been raised to leave people with a polite pleasantry, and his upbringing didn't fail him, not even in this dire moment. I wanted to reach through my radio and hug the guy.

Mothers in my patch of the Midwest defined a code of behavior by three admonitions: "Stop staring at people." "Don't ask so many questions." And "If you can't say something nice, don't say anything at all." I don't remember *my* mother ever saying those things, but by just walking through our lives we picked them up, like slang and scabby knees and chigger bites. Could there be worse guidance for someone later to become a writer?

Not that I was conscious, growing up, of any literary intent. I was pretty much devoid of all intent until I was twenty-one years old, unless wanting to be left alone adds up to intent. But when I look back, I see that in my childhood were three skeins waiting to be braided into writer's cord. First was my love of reading, from cereal boxes to Dr. Seuss to *The Boxcar Children* to boys' baseball books to *Escape from Warsaw* to science fiction to Bruce Catton on the Civil War to anything bound between covers. My father, who lives alone at age eighty-five in the house I grew up in, recently showed me a carousel of slides he'd put together. The photographs document twenty years of me and my late mother, and in picture after picture, no matter what is going on around me, I am off to the side or in a corner reading. In the fourth grade, my elementary school ran a battery of tests and declared that I was reading at the eleventh-grade level. By the time I was twelve, I had my own copy of Plato's *Republic.* I never read it, but I meant to, and that's the point.

The second skein was a native ability to make sentences. I don't know where I got it, it was just there. In school, term papers and essay questions were never hard. When I was in junior high, now called middle school, the local American Legion post sponsored a contest for essays about the American flag. I wasn't interested until my English teacher offered extra credit. I still wasn't sufficiently interested to re-member the essay until the morning it was due, whereupon I took up my pen and in the fifteen minutes of homeroom before class I dashed off a few pages. The essay won the ninth-grade prize, a pen-and-pencil set inscribed AMERICANISM AWARD. After the meeting of the Legion where we read our winning efforts, the mother of the triumphant eighth-grader fixed a cold, suspicious gaze on me and said, "Did your parents help you with that?"

The last skein was an odd delight, evident at a young age, in showing people how they really are. One year for Christmas my mom and dad gave me a tape recorder. Soon I put it to use by hiding it during parties at our house, recording the banter and the laughter. Nothing was more fun than that moment when I revealed the hidden device, then played the tape for all the grown-ups, who inevitably were embarrassed by the tim-bre of their voices and the harsh loudness of their cackling. They were always good-natured about it, but I could sense the discomfort under their amusement, and that fascinated me. I liked being the cause of it.

But never would I have become a writer had I not left Mt. Healthy for Athens. When the kid who had enjoyed hiding tape recorders en-tered college, he was sober, sheltered, and uninitiated, with nothing to say. Four years away from home changed that. Athens and Ohio Univer-sity were hardly Greenwich Village West or the Far Left Bank. But com-ing from my background, I might as well have been a little shepherd boy who'd just strolled into Sodom and Gomorrah. College provided op-portunities to train the intellect and broaden one's horizons, and I did both. It also provided opportunities to get drunk, get high, and get laid, and I did all of that, too, with varying degrees of fumbling tentativeness. A few years into my undergraduate studies, I returned home for a visit. Just before I headed back to campus, my mother looked at my father and said, "That is *not* the boy we sent away."

Actually, for the first year I *was* the boy they sent away, earnest and studious, on the dean's list and still dating my hometown sweetheart. But at the start of my sophomore year, I joined the staff of the student newspaper, and life became what my mother would have called a whole 'nuther thing. My new friends had bleary eyes, pasty complexions, and a fondness for staying up all night. They smoked cigarettes, they smoked marijuana, they drank beer and Boone's Farm wine and tequila, they listened to rock 'n' roll, and they all wanted to be writers. They were the coolest people I'd ever met, and I wanted to be one of them.

Here was a new way to live, and it felt deliciously bohemian. The choices I had! If I wanted to walk the rain-slicked streets at four in the morning, the solitary poetic brooder, I could. If I wanted to sit in an all-night donut shop, sip acid coffee, smoke mentholated cigarillos, and discuss Kurt Vonnegut or Hunter S. Thompson or Hermann Hesse, I could. I could try out being literary, and self-destructive in an artsy sort of way, and nobody would tell me to stop. People who read the *Village Voice* and talked revolutionary politics and took amphetamines to fuel another twelve hours of typing and conversation surrounded me. So did theater and art and film and concerts and alternative newspapers and underground comics and campus radicals. There were easily obtained intoxicants and no end of pretty girls, some of whom would share a bottle of Mateus Portuguese wine with you and then take off their clothes. So long, Mt. Healthy, it's been good to know ya.

My habits changed from attending every class and studying in the library every night, with review sessions on Sunday mornings, to ignoring my course schedule and sleeping until noon, when I slept at all. Instead of going to class, I'd hole up in the library with bound original editions of *Scribner's* or the *Saturday Evening Post*, reading Hemingway and Fitzgerald and plotting how I was going to beat them at their own game. I discovered literary journals like the *Paris Review,* and scrutinized interviews with novelists and poets, looking for the magic keys. In my knapsack I toted a copy of John Berryman's *The Dream Songs.* I worked my way through D. H. Lawrence and Jack Kerouac, *Zen and the Art of Motorcycle Maintenance* and *The Glass Bead Game.* I began writing a novel, and every day I wrote column inch after column inch for the student newspaper, thrilled to feed a spool of teletype paper through an upright Underwood, just like Kerouac, self-important in my role as a member of the Watergate-era press. We had brought down a government, by god, and on a local note managed to piss off the university's administration at every turn. We were journalists, and we spoke truth to power. Gonzo, baby, and did you say that term paper was due *last* week?

All this undergraduate dissipation turned into something when I encountered Daniel Keyes. I don't think he has many readers these days, but back then *Flowers for Algernon* was a big deal and Keyes was the most famous writer I'd ever known. I enrolled in his fiction workshop at the start of my senior year and walked in as a cocky twenty-one-year-old, skeptical that anyone could improve on my talent. Within two classes, Keyes made it clear that as far he was concerned, not only could I not write, I could barely read. His great gift as a teacher was the ability to deliver this verdict but not discourage me or make me so mad I quit the course. Instead, he lit me up. After only a few weeks of his tutelage, I wanted nothing more than to become a great writer. I am still at it today because of him.

I didn't know it, but while I was in Athens an internal dialogue had begun, a dialogue of contending influences that shaped the writer emerging from the callow boy. From my hometown came a lasting instinct for plain speech and a dislike of too much adornment or self-indulgent cleverness. I retained a regard for traditional forms and a suspicion of theory and the avant-garde. The sentimentality and comfortable blandness and witless fallback to conventional wisdom had to go, but I kept the deadpan wit and the tendency toward good manners. I also kept my identification with the working class. From my college town came a measure of bad manners plus a lasting disdain for authority, a fondness for sarcasm, a reflexive skepticism, and a profound respect for the artist's, and the journalist's, duty to speak truth.

I never quite fit in either place, but that's good for a writer. Nor did I ever become a novelist. My talents just don't run along that path. But, as Paul Theroux once put it, I've been writing with both hands every workday for most of my adult life, and I don't want to do anything else. Our parents used to warn us not to overdo it. Well, I like people who overdo it, and ever since college I've been one of them. And I still enjoy pissing off the administration. Any administration will do. For fifteen years now I've been an Easterner, but though the boy left the Midwest, the Midwest has not left the boy. My two Ohio towns still jockey for influence, like two sides of an opinionated family. But that's all right. Power to the people, fuck the system, and hey, have a nice day and tell your mom I said hi.

about the author

Despite habits of dissipation and a lack of direction, DALE KEIGER graduated summa cum laude from the Scripps School of Journalism at Ohio University in 1976. He worked in Cincinnati for ten years as a freelance journalist, publishing in the *Washington Post*, the *Los Angeles Times*, *Connoisseur*, *Travel and Leisure*, and many other publications, including Major League Baseball's all-star game program. For his reporting on the Keating savings and loan scandal in 1989, he won a *Washington Monthly* national journalism prize and an H. L. Mencken Award for investigative reporting.

Since 1992, Keiger has been a senior writer at *Johns Hopkins Magazine*. He teaches graduate nonfiction writing workshops at Johns Hopkins University. After fifteen years in Baltimore, where he resides with his wife, Marian Grant, he remains a fan—albeit a frustrated fan—of the Cincinnati Reds.

This Is the Place

Julie Salamon

SEAMAN

Julie Salamon, center, with her mother, sister, and pups, 1958

MY PARENTS, SURVIVORS OF AUSCHWITZ

and Dachau concentration camps, were from Czechoslovakia. In 1953, having spent several years in New York, they moved to southern Ohio with their four-year-old daughter, my sister. My mother was seven months pregnant with me.

The Promised Land comes in many guises. Moses stared across the desert and declared it the land of milk and honey. Marty Weiss thought it was Miami Beach. Sanyi Salamon, my father, decided his land of milk and honey was here, the western outpost of Appalachia.

He knew nothing about this place he had decided to fall in love with. That, for example, this county that at one time had occupied a quarter of the state now wavered between being the poorest and the second poorest of Ohio's eighty-eight counties. That fewer than 5 percent of its high school graduates went on to college or even thought about it. That it was sixty miles from Cincinnati, a two-hour drive on stomach-shaking roads, and the geographic distance was small compared to the cultural distance.

He couldn't see up into the hills, where people still believed in both the devil and moonshine, though the county was officially "dry," having declined to join the rest of the country's repeal of Prohibition twenty years before—a state of affairs that worked to the mutual satisfaction of both the bootleggers and the preachers. The only industry was farming, mostly small family farms handed down from generation to generation.

He didn't know he'd be the only Jew in town, one of a handful in the entire county—nor that his religion wouldn't matter to most of the townspeople, who were much more suspicious of Catholics (but who would casually use the expression "I jewed him down" as a way of saying they'd gotten something at a cheaper price). Yet the homogeneity of the citizenry—almost entirely white Protestant—didn't alleviate the paranoia that prevailed across the county, where it was said if six people gathered together they'd start a town, build a church, and start gossiping suspiciously about their neighbors.

It was a peculiar place, geographically remote and geologically interesting, the place where Ohio burst out of its northern flatness into hills and ridges. Hundreds of thousands of years before, the glacier out of Canada that had rolled the northern United States flat had stopped in Adams

County, forever changing its landscape. The foothills of the Appalachian Mountains began there, and so did the fertile soil of the Kentucky bluegrass region. Its plants and fossils, revealing millions of years of evolution, were periodically studied by scientists from Cincinnati but were of scant interest to the local inhabitants. Indeed, with Baptist fundamentalism as the prevailing religion, evolution was a subject best avoided.

People in Adams County didn't care much about the world outside. Until World War II, it was said, you could count on one hand the number of people who had ever been out of the county. They even spoke a special dialect because people came there, got stuck, and never heard anything else.

They sustained themselves on their homegrown beauty and bigotry. Their accents and prejudices were vaguely southern, but their heritage was northern. A man could use the word "nigger" in the same sentence as he noted with pride that Adams County had been the first stop to freedom on the Underground Railroad. The few black people who lived in the county were not fully accepted, nor were they abused—but that was pretty much the way Adams Countians treated everyone who hadn't lived there for six generations. Serious disdain was much more insular— saved by Methodists for Presbyterians and by residents of Peebles for residents of Blue Creek.

Sanyi saw none of that, or chose not to see it. What he saw was a sky so clear he felt it was possible to see every star in the galaxy, the end of a rainbow. "It's a nice little town with friendly people," he said when he returned to New York, by way of explaining to Szimi, my mother, why she should leave her friends and family and move to the middle of nowhere just before their second baby was due.

Szimi arrived by train in Ohio on May 21, 1953, almost nine years to the day after her arrival in Auschwitz. At a gas station just outside the train station, she was staring idly out the car window when she saw a man leading on a rope a beautiful black-and-white creature with a luxurious tail. She opened the car door and stood up to get a better look.

"Don't make him angry, or he'll let you have it," said the man holding the rope.

She smiled because he was smiling, and he must have seen that she didn't know what he was talking about.

"Haven't you ever seen a skunk, ma'am?" he asked. He explained how skunks let loose a foul smell when they are upset.

"Amazing," Szimi said, as she mentally transformed this encounter into yet another symbol of life's extraordinary serendipity. It must be a sign, she was sure of it. What else could explain this introduction to an animal she hadn't know existed just as she arrived in Ohio—especially an animal like that, a soft, furry thing with secret powers of survival. She was prepared to believe, once again, that her new life was beginning.

YEARS LATER, PRUDIE COOPER would remember the arrival of Alexander and Lilly Salamon, as Sanyi and Szimi would become known, with a sense of drama and portent that clearly indicated why she and Lilly became such good friends.

Prudie was short and stubby and always seemed to be flying, partly because her little legs had to work twice as hard as a normal-sized person's to get where she was going as fast as she wanted. Her estimation, that the doctor's arrival was a miracle, wasn't altered by the fact that the miracle wouldn't take place until a year after the Salamons came to town.

She was baking an angel food cake for a friend when Chip came down, waxy faced, saying his arms were hurting. Prudie called Dr. Salamon, whose office was just down the road. He came right over to the house, took one look at Chip, and told him to go to bed.

"You go ahead and bake your cake," he told Prudie. "I'll see to it everything's all right." And though Chip had had a heart attack, Doc Salamon did see to it that everything was all right, for the longest time.

Like many people in Adams County, which sat on the Ohio River just north of Kentucky, Prudie had been born in Kentucky and spoke with a twang that was part southern, part country. Her family had ended up in Adams County when her father had traded some homes he'd built in Dayton for a farm someone had owned in Adams County. This was a common sort of phenomenon in Adams County, a place people didn't usually head toward but landed in.

Prudie married young and started having babies with the boy everyone called Chip. Prudie had an irrepressible bent for self-improvement that eventually would lead her to a political career trying to convince state officials that Adams County was not just a backwater full of poor, ignorant people.

She would never forget Dr. Salamon's arrival. "The Lions Club was really interested in getting a doctor in town, but truthfully, no one wanted to put out the money for the building and the house. I got a call from Socks Roush, the president of the Lions, who said the doctor from New York was in Hamersville and would like to come down but he needed to know he'd have a permanent place. Socks wanted to know if Chip would put up the money.

"I called every automobile agency in Dayton where I thought he might be, and finally I found him. He said, 'We can't afford all ten thousand dollars, but I'll put in five if the building and loan will put up the rest.'"

In a later age it would be said that anyone can reach anyone in just six calls. In Seaman, whose population in 1953 was 714, it didn't take six calls. Everyone knew everyone else. Prudie called the banker and Socks Roush called the hardware store owner, and they all waited for the doctor to arrive. When he did, Socks sent him over to Prudie's house and she told him to come back for supper.

"The Lions Club agreed to put up money to renovate the building because they knew he was coming here with practically nothing," she recalled. "I think that's what they wanted. I think they wanted someone who didn't have anything."

Prudie began to think about what to make for dinner. She realized she didn't know what nationality Dr. Salamon was, but she thought he might be Jewish. She served on the Ladies' Auxiliary at the hospital, and when they had regional meetings they made sure not to serve ham because they understood it was against the religion of the Jewish doctors. Just to be safe, she decided to make chicken.

That evening she had the kids scrubbed and waiting on the porch when he drove up in a light blue Oldsmobile with a dark green roof. The children couldn't stop staring at this big, dark man wearing a jacket and tie and a white shirt.

They followed the adults into the kitchen and sat in their chairs barely breathing, they were so quiet. The doctor didn't seem to notice them at all until suddenly each of them, one by one, felt him reaching across their shoulders, leaving something on the table by every plate. They stared at these little round contraptions dumbfounded, just the way they'd been staring at him.

"Do you have milk in your glasses?" the doctor asked.

They nodded, eyes wide.

He reached over and turned over one of the boxes.

"*Moooo,*" it went.

The children looked at him, then at the box, their tense little mouths now smiling.

"I brought you the cows!" he said.

Their fascination with this stranger escalated during dinner. While they picked up their fried chicken to get at the meat near the bone, the doctor dissected his neatly with his knife and fork. They left half their meals, they were so absorbed in the doctor's technique, the way he managed to pick off every last shred without getting a drop of grease on his hands.

After dinner the children were excused from the table and Dr. Salamon began to talk, very fast, until he must have noticed from the expression on Prudie and Chip's faces that they were only catching every third word.

He slowed down and told him what he thought they needed to know. He told them about his wife.

"She's no bigger than you," he said to Prudie, smiling, putting his hand low in the air. "She's pregnant like you"—he held his hand way out in front of his stomach—"only bigger. I told her she ate so much watermelon she must have swallowed a seed and was growing one inside."

He told them that he was from Czechoslovakia and that during the war he had been in a concentration camp. Prudie remembered distinctly that when her face tightened in sorrow for him, he was quick to assure her that he had got more privileges than he might have because he was a doctor. He told her that "they" had come one night and taken his father and mother—or so he understood—but he had never learned exactly what happened.

It became clear to her as he talked that he wasn't asking for pity but was trying to emphasize his credentials. "When I went back to where I lived, there was an ash pile behind the house," he told them. "On top of that ash pile was a long cardboard tube, and in it was my medical diploma, unharmed. I was fortunate that it lay there and refused to burn because it gave me distinct proof that I had a diploma."

That was all he had to say about his past, except to mention that he had once played the violin. When he finished talking, he looked at Chip and said, "Shall we go take a look?"

As they drove up the road toward the house, Dr. Salamon said, "They really wanted me in Hamersville, but I couldn't go there. They were widening the roads and cutting down the big trees. I thought to myself, 'You know, I could not live in a place where the big trees were destroyed.'"

He didn't mention the unenthusiastic reception he'd gotten at the Georgetown Hospital, near Hamersville.

When they got to the lot, the trees around the buildings, which had been bare on his first visit, were bursting with leaves. Dr. Salamon spent a few minutes inside the house, then wandered out back. After some time he joined Prudie and Chip by the car.

"Aren't they gorgeous?" he asked, gesturing vaguely at the woods.

They felt the words weren't directed at them. He looked up at the sky, lit by a last golden burst before nightfall, and repeated, "I just couldn't live somewhere where they would cut down the big trees."

Back at the house they were sitting outside talking, watching the sun go down, when a skinny little old man came running up, panting.

"Someone said they's a doctor here. That right?" he asked.

Prudie and Chip weren't surprised to see him. In a town like Seaman, news of a stranger's arrival at one end of town would reach the other end of town before he did. They introduced Dr. Salamon to the agitated old man.

"Come with me," he said to the doctor. "I got a friend up the road who's really sick. Needs help bad."

The doctor got up to follow the old man without asking him a thing. As he left he thanked Prudie for supper, and the evening was over. They didn't know where he stayed that night.

Prudie and Chip, who had spent most of their lives in Adams County, didn't take unusual appearances by strangers lightly. They had the feeling that they'd witnessed something momentous. Prudie would say of that night, "It reminded me of Brigham Young when he got to Utah and said, 'This is the place.'"

SUZY, AGE FOUR AND a half, sitting in the backseat, was disgusted as she listened to her parents exclaiming about everything: how beautiful the trees were, how fine the house would be when the walls were up and when the mess in the backyard was put into order. Couldn't they see what she saw? That there was nothing but huge piles of dirt because the town didn't have a sewage system and a septic tank had to be installed for indoor plumbing?

She hated this place. At home in New York she'd had friends to play with in the daytime and so many grown-ups who loved her around at night. She missed Baba, more patient than her mother, who would let her sit in the bath as long as she wanted and read stories to her.

Here, she and Mommy spent all day just sitting outside watching men pounding and digging while her father went off to work somewhere. Once in a while they would sit on a bench in front of the dry-goods store in the unbearable heat. They were always thirsty. She heard her mother complain to her father one night that when she had asked one of the neighbors where she could get a drink, the woman had told her there was a soda machine in the little knife factory across the street. What kind of people were these?

Suzy didn't care to find out. It was too hot and the air was too thick. She wanted to go home.

For three days she refused to eat anything but a spoonful of ice cream. When her father asked her what was wrong, she looked at him angrily and asked, precociously, "How could you drag me away to a strange land? Why are you breaking my heart?"

Szimi could see Sanyi was wounded by Suzy's words, unreasonably so, though she didn't tell him that. She was concerned, too, but not *unreasonably* so. "Sure enough," she would say triumphantly, "on the fourth day, Suzy's hunger strike ended."

People emerged from the house in the middle of the woods next door, specifically a woman who seemed to have something pulling on her skirts. A face surrounded by a head of curls emerged to stare shyly at the newcomers. The two little girls appraised each other warily while their mothers introduced themselves. Belva Beery, the Baptist mission-ary's wife, chatted with Lilly Salamon, the Jewish doctor's wife, as their daughters bridged the gap between city and country and ran off into the woods. At lunchtime Mrs. Beery invited Suzy to have lunch with her new friend Annette. That evening Suzy declared to her parents that apple dumplings was the best thing she'd ever eaten.

SZIMI WOULD EVENTUALLY LEARN how to make apple dumplings, though her menus would remain primarily Czech and Hungarian. Her children would grow up eating navy beans and ham, mashed potatoes and gravy, and tuna casserole at their friends' houses and food with mysterious names at home, dishes like chicken *paprikas, lecsó, knedle, shliskele.*

Eventually she would accept her position as the town exotic, but in those early days she concentrated on ordinariness. This would have been the biggest stretch of all for her powers of adaptation even if she hadn't always seen herself as extremely . . . unusual. It seemed to her that ordinariness required a working knowledge of predictability, and it had been a long time since she'd counted predictability among her standards of measure. It was difficult to plan ahead when you didn't know where you would be tomorrow.

Yet when she drove down Main Street in Seaman for the first time with her husband and child, Szimi saw that this was a place where peo-ple knew where they'd been and could predict where they were going. She suspected she had reached a place where the striking of lightning was an exception, not the rule.

about the author

JULIE SALAMON has been a staff critic, essayist, and reporter for the *New York Times* and a film critic for the *Wall Street Journal.*

Her books are varied. *The Devil's Candy* (Houghton Mifflin, 1991) looks at big-budget Hollywood movie-making. Since then her books have taken her many places. In *The Net of Dreams* (Random House, 1996), she retraces her parents' journey from the Carpathian Mountains to the Appalachian foothills via Dachau and Auschwitz. She has written a novella about the Rockefeller Center Christmas tree. *Facing the Wind* (Random House, 2001) is a nonfiction account of a killing that involved women with blind children, a father who appeared to rise above difficulty, and how their lives met at the intersection of mental illness, innocence, and retribution. Her most recent book is *Rambam's Ladder* (Workman, 2003), a reported rumination that connects the teachings of the twelfth-century philosopher Maimonides with the complexities of modern-day philanthropy.

Salamon is the daughter of Hungarian Jews, the only Jews in Seaman, Ohio, a town of 800 otherwise populated by Southern Baptists, Methodists, and a smattering of Presbyterians. Her parents, survivors of the Holocaust, presented their two daughers with a daunting example: how to remember the great evil done to them and their families while approaching life with hopefulness and compassion. Writing may not have been inevitable, but it became for Salamon essential.

Heroes and Tree Huts

James Toedtman

BEREA

Jimmy Toedtman, age five, in 1946

IN MY CHILDHOOD MEMORIES, LIFE

began in a tree. Our tree hut straddled the second ring of tree limbs in the apple tree by the back alley. From my perch fifteen feet above the ground, I could see smoke from the Ford plant and watch planes from Cleveland Hopkins Airport. I could hear trains on the fourteen east-west tracks passing through town. I had a bird's-eye view of the family vegetable garden and through windows on two sides could see the campus of Baldwin-Wallace College.

There, I learned to dream.

At the beginning of the twenty-first century, it all seems magical—our special neighborhood, the college next door with its fields and students, ballgames that lasted for days, the early discipline of a paper route, the inspiration of an Olympic champion. Those dynamics defined growing up in Berea, Ohio, in the years after World War II, and the lessons endure.

Labeled Cleveland's "reluctant suburb," Berea straddled the line where Cleveland sprawl met the fading, blurred edge of rural Ohio. Berea's reluctance grew from its history as a sandstone-quarrying town, its downtown Triangle where we gathered for parades and celebrations, and its allure as the home of Baldwin-Wallace. With this commercial and cultural identity, Berea resisted the relentless pull of the colossus to the north.

This was the heartland of industrial America, and many in Berea worked shifts at the Cadillac tank plant or the nearby Ford foundry and assembly plant. Cleveland's ever-growing presence in the life of Berea manifested itself as more and more of our fathers, including my dad, commuted to the Republic and Jones and Laughlin steel mills, the banks, the clothing stores, and the commercial offices in the city.

Growing up was notable for the protection that our town and our neighborhood provided. Within two blocks lived five families and a dozen kids who grew up together, explored, camped, learned, played, and fought together. This was long before the era of organized play, which meant our parents left us to learn these lessons pretty much on our own. We experimented with crystal radios, chemistry sets, and tin cans on a string. We staged our own circuses and celebrated the first television in the neighborhood, gathering around it each afternoon for the test pattern, then Uncle Jake, then Howdy Doody, then the news and the test pattern.

Except for basketball, which knew no season, games depended on the time of year. Spring and summer baseball games continued from one day to the next. We shared gloves, mimicked our beloved Cleveland Indians—Jim Hegan was my favorite—and tossed the bat for picking teams and first bats. If baseball's a game of situation, we learned the situations then. See Manny Ramirez batting with two runners in scoring position, and I know how he feels. We lived next to the college's practice football field, which meant our games each autumn were squeezed between the end of school and the beginning of the college team's regular drills. It also meant that we found part-time work as wide-eyed if unofficial assistants to Frank "Digger" Dawson (now an East Liverpool undertaker), the Yellow Jackets student manager. We strapped shoulder pads, collected hundreds of rolls of tape, sorted helmets, folded home and away jerseys. And we tossed the football.

Our Schwinns and Roadmasters, with timely assists from Clarence Fox's bicycle shop, provided our primary transportation. Campus sidewalks became our highways. It seems we rode for days, through territory bounded by our frontiers—the Triangle and the Point, about three miles apart. But Berea's special gift was its location and the perspective it provided as we heard the haunting steam whistles of giant locomotives connecting Cleveland to Detroit and Chicago, Cincinnati, and Buffalo.

Overhead, we watched the jet age emerge. We shared the excitement of the annual Cleveland air races and watched experimental airplanes, prop-driven, then turbo props, World War II Corvairs, and the unusual "Flying Wings" circling over the airfield. Even though my first flight was still a decade away, I lived under the Cleveland flight path and dreamed of faraway destinations like New York and Washington. One friend's father worked at NASA's Lewis Lab, where the nation's fledgling space program was being hatched. Another friend's mother worked for Northwest Orient Airlines, a link to exotic places like Minneapolis, Vancouver, and over the Pacific Ocean.

The 100 Club captured the magic of my childhood in Ohio. Ted Theodore, then a middle-distance runner for Baldwin-Wallace and a hero because he found time for the neighborhood kids, created the club. Collecting autographs was probably a Cub Scout project as I worked the crowd at one of the AAU track meets held each summer at the college track. When I asked for his autograph, Ted took my little yellow tablet and neatly wrote across the top, "100 Club." That set the target: Collect a hundred signatures.

Today the pages are in my scrapbook, fifty-five years older, with dry, faded colors and tattered edges. By my count, the signatures include three Olympic champions, three NFL stars (including two Hall of Famers), five college coaches, and two NFL coaches. Not to mention Bud Collins, the great storyteller of our childhood and now a tennis commentator, and Bob Beach, then a student, later a writer and public relations man and as influential a mentor as I ever had.

Lou "the Toe" Groza, another signer, thrilled dozens of neighborhood children from me to Ohio State University head football coach Jim Tressel by letting us shag his practice kicks every summer on the practice fields. For two years, I ghostwrote a column for Lou, who remained a family friend until his death. But my memories of him were forged chasing his kicks and then cleaning his square-toed shoes in the locker room of the Baldwin-Wallace stadium.

In the music section of the 100 Club, Edwin Franco Goldman—then one of the world's celebrated musicians and a guest conductor at the college—signed. So did Frederick Ebbs, director of the marching band at Baldwin-Wallace and later at Iowa and Indiana—despite our tendency to disrupt his band practices with errant football kicks into the middle of his band's formations.

The college provided opportunity for mischief (like the time we drove the college tractor around the practice field until it ran out of gas) and adventure (biking at super speeds across the campus). Even for kids, it provided challenge. Inside the field house where we often played, we passed a wall mural with the admonition "It is easy to be ordinary, but takes courage to excel, And we must excel." I first saw the rings of Saturn from the college observatory's telescope. Jim Lawson, a student and 100 Club signer, left Berea and became a devotee of Gandhi, a confidant of Martin Luther King, and leader of the civil rights movement that would dominate our lives.

Then there was the *Berea News*, the town's weekly newspaper. My tale of our gang's efforts to save a baby bunny stuck under a pile of lumber at the college quonset huts produced my first byline as a third-grader, launching my career in journalism. I didn't realize it at the time, but my morning paper route affirmed my career choice. I experienced the thrill of discovering new facts—from the Browns' scores and Indians' batting averages to the death of Josef Stalin—before others. My *Plain Dealer* customers likely grumbled. But huddling over a stack of papers in the predawn darkness, I devoured every nugget in every column every day. Only then, filled with the latest news, would I start down the alley to Beech Street and begin to share it.

For perspective, I had the tree hut. It was an apple tree, with springtime blossoms, then green saplings, which we cut and used for flinging young apples as far as we could see. In summer we picked sweet and sour apples for snacks, sauce, and apple pie. And in fall, the apples ripened for pressing into cider—and for raking.

We built our hut with two roughly parallel limbs, two two-by-four crossbars, and loosely fitted walls. The roof we adapted from a plywood box that had once wrapped a casket (we had salvaged it from the trash pile behind Baker's Funeral Home on Front Street). Of the hut's many redeeming features, the most notable may have been the lack of a single 90-degree angle. It served many purposes, meeting our needs as an airplane cabin, an escape, a hideaway, and a headquarters, depending on the adventure of the day.

The hut produced its inglorious moments too. Once, with visions of Icarus the Greek aerialist, we strapped on a plastic playpen cover, assuming it would open and become a parachute. It didn't. One friend fell and broke his collarbone. I got tangled in branches on the way down and hung suspended for several minutes until gravity prevailed, and I discovered the unyielding nature of Mother Earth.

The hut is long gone. But the lessons have endured.

It is to Ohio where my memory turns, providing a constant point of reference. The scale has changed, and a lifetime of travel, a far-flung family, and interesting work have forced many adjustments. But it is in Ohio where the essential alignment of the compass was set. I prize loyalty and my family. I feel enriched by the blessings of nature. I treasure friendship. I have been inspired not to accept defeat without looking for the next opportunity. If the prevailing message delivered constantly by my mother was "remember who you are," the prevailing message in the years since has been "remember where you're from."

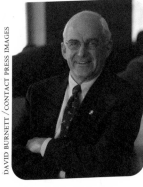

DAVID BURNETT / CONTACT PRESS IMAGES

about the author

A veteran journalist, newspaper editor, and Pulitzer Prize–winning team member, JAMES TOEDTMAN is editor of *AARP Bulletin*. Before that appointment in 2005, he worked for *Newsday* for thirty-two years, serving as managing editor responsible for the production of the paper's New York City edition and later as Washington bureau chief and chief economics correspondent. Toedtman was also executive editor of the *Boston Herald American* and editor of the *Baltimore News American*.

He earned his undergraduate degree from the College of Wooster and his master's degree from Columbia University's School of Journalism. He studied at the University of Queensland, Australia, as a Rotary Foundation Fellow. In 1970 he shared a Pulitzer Prize for a series of Long Island land scandals and in 1992 for spot news reporting of the New York City subway crash. His other honors include a first-place award from the Maryland-Delaware-DC Press Association and an honorable mention from the Inter-American Press Association. He is a guest lecturer at Flagler College in St. Augustine, Florida. Toedtman lives in Oakton, Virginia, with his wife. They have two children.

Decoction

Mark Winegardner

BRYAN

Mark Winegardner celebrating his third birthday in 1964 between his father and mother

I GREW UP IN A TWO-STORY BRICK

house that never had an onion in it.

(I'm exaggerating. First of all, two other families lived in that house before we did, and I can't speak to their attitudes vis-à-vis the pungent onion. Also, I didn't live in that house until I was seven. Before that, I lived in a double-wide house *trailer*, on the edge of town. A cornfield separated us from the trailer court my grandfather owned, operated, and sold most of the trailers into. We bought corn at the store anyway, usually in cans. Why we didn't just swipe it from that field—which, after all, belonged to my grandfather—is one of the mysteries of my childhood. Another one is why my mother, now staunchly liberal, voted for Richard Nixon three times. I'm also unclear about [a] why, when we did move into a real house, that brick one in town, we gave away my dog Scamp; [b] what I was so hacked off about that made me fight so much with my little sister Shari; and [c] why my father never kept beer in the house.)

I was born and raised in a small town in northwesternmost Ohio—Bryan, home of the Dum-Dum Sucker—in a house that never had a clove of garlic in it. Our house never contained any spices other than salt (crystalline NaCl, not an actual spice), pepper (even a blind chicken finds the rare kernel of peppercorn), sugar (a water-soluble crystalline carbohydrate, also not a true spice), and the dull, sweet brown ones my mother used for a few days each fall, to bake apple and pumpkin pies. In my house, curry would have been more exotic than heroin.

(Again I'm invoking a fraudulently obtained poetic license. Fact is, the spices were kept in the liquor cabinet, which was built into the pantry: two shelves high, two feet wide, and lockable. It contained rarely employed containers of garlic powder, vodka, rum, onion powder, crème de menthe, and this one tiny, forlorn tin of stale Kroger's-brand chili powder, which survived the entirety of my childhood. My father drank, but not the booze. Warm, incomplete fifteen-packs of Stroh's, purchased because it came with three extra cans for the same price as most twelve-packs, were hidden in the garage and the basement and under mossy logs in the woodpile out back. My father neither ate nor drank for taste. My mother did; she liked the limey haze of vodka gimlets, but had maybe five a year. The most threatening thing in that liquor cabinet was the chili powder. On those giddy occasions when someone had an impulse to add a pinch of it to some bland meat-based thing simmering bleakly atop the avocado green range, my mother would say, "Careful, careful!" After I got out of college I helped my parents move to a house in a town eighteen miles south of there—Defiance, the least aptly named town in Ohio [the most? Chagrin Falls]. Still is. The trailer dealership that my grandfather had started in the 1930s, and that my parents had bought from him in the early seventies and presided over during the lingering demise of, was called Winegardner Mobile Homes. Was. My mother, who'd taught herself bookkeeping so she could keep that cost in family, saved her and my father's bacon by landing a cost-accounting job at a big factory in Defiance. My father became an insurance agent, although, broken by the failure of the business his father had started, he spent almost every day driving to Fort Wayne and going to the movies, having an affair with Twizzlers, vats of popcorn, and whatever Hollywood sent to the Southtown Mall Cineplex, rather than with another woman, like a normal father would have. The day I packed up my parents' kitchen, that thing of chili powder was still there. There was about a quarter of it left. The Kroger's where it was purchased had gone belly-up—fourteen years earlier than Winegardner Mobile Homes.)

Here's what meals were like in the spiceless, unseasoned house of my youth. My parents would come home from work. Typically this would mean my mother emerging haggard from the back-bedroom home office, tired and drawn from the hopeless state of the trailer sales' finances, and my father returning home from the sales lot in an oil-dripping, company-owned Chevy Suburban. Sometimes, though, my mother would be at the lot, too; sometimes my father snuck out of work and spent the afternoon with his metal detector, digging up pop tabs in a park someplace. Wherever. They would meet in the kitchen. One of them would unwrap the pound of hamburger that had been thawing all day in the sink. Stove on. Teflon skillet out (a lighter shade of avocado green than the range top).

Plop the meat in the skillet. Remove the Styrofoam thing.

Brown the meat.

Then, and only then, figure out what's going to go in it.

One favorite: a family-sized can of baked beans, augmented with a cup of ketchup (not a vegetable) and a half-cup of brown sugar (not a spice). Stir well. Serve hot.

That was one of the good ones.

Often, if a "recipe" failed to occur to them, they would pour in a can of tomato sauce (the kind with other stuff in it, including spices, hadn't yet been invented) and keep thinking.

Some of the things they decided to put with it might, in these more enlightened times, constitute child abuse. On more than one occasion they stirred in a bagful of frozen vegetables. Peas. Peas and carrots. Corn. Lima beans.

This would be served up with no apology, on harvest gold-trimmed Corelle dinner plates, ladled so full the trim was submerged.

"What is it?" I would often say.

"Chili," my mother would say. "Eat it."

My mother and father would discuss their doomed efforts to keep their mom-and-pop small-town trailer sales afloat.

"He made a face at me!" my sister would say.

"I did not," I'd say, and kick her under the table.

"Ow!" she'd say. If they had not been watching us, she'd claim that I'd hit her in the eye, which always got me in more trouble, typically a spanking with a handsome wooden paddle that had been left behind in a traded-in trailer. (I realize now that it was the sort of paddle designed to give pleasure to masochistic adults, but my parents wouldn't have recognized it as such.)

"He hit me in the eye!" she'd say.

"Are you going to eat that?" my father would say after I'd been spanked.

"Yes," I'd say. Terrible food, and the helpings too small.

(I'm not being fair. First of all, by the standards of the place and time I grew up, my parents' cooking wasn't so different than my friends' parents.' Second, if I'm honest—which, let's face it, we can never be, with the past; truth is a parenthetical component of memory—I don't remember thinking at the time about how horrible the food was. This reflects badly on me, not them, and, to compensate, I have spent my adult life eating as much spicy and/or exquisite food as I can. Third, *nothing* my parents could have done would have saved that business; *all* small-town mom-and-pop trailer sales died in the seventies, flushed to oblivion alongside the eight-track tape and unironic patriotism. Fourth, as I cannot stress enough, my mother baked fine pies. Still does. Fifth, when my father finally joined AA, which in fact happened four years before his business went under, I was surprised; I do not have a single true memory of him being drunk. Finally, I have created the impression that chili-free "chili" was all we ever ate. It wasn't. To vary our menus they also performed analogous feats on boxed Kraft mac'n'cheese and called those "casseroles." Try it. Important stir-ins include peas, tuna fish, undiluted cans of either Campbell's tomato or Campbell's cream of mushroom soup, or some unholy combination thereof. Dinners that did not feature "chili" or "casseroles": tartare-centered, burned-crisp hamburgers or steak, gas-grilled while my father inspected the woodpile; dishes involving Miracle Whip; Raisin Bran; instant mashed potatoes baked over a layer of canned corn and a layer of browned meat; oven-burned steroid-fed chicken, treated with preservative-laden Shake 'n Bake [and I helped]. Plus, there was always room for Jell-O. While I am plumbing lies for truth, I should also say that my father, sober and thus sans the attractive nuisance of warm beer in the woodpile, continued to burn all grilled meat to ash.)

God bless the miraculous advent of Hamburger Helper: boxed, salty, noodley, cheesy, the same every time. *Hamburger Helper / Helps your hamburger,* went the product's TV jingle, *Help you / Make a great meal.*

Help had arrived. We tried every variety the supermarket stocked.

By that time I had taken the PSAT test. Fat, glossy college catalogs came daily in the mail. Many of these featured happy, pretty people just a little older than I was, eating in their dining halls with no adult supervision. The food looked great!

* * *

"Once I had recognized the taste of the crumb of madeleine soaked in the decoction of lime flowers which my aunt used to give me, immediately the old gray house upon the street, where her room was, rose up like the scenery of a theater . . ."

Proust made a bigger deal of all this than anyone, of course—a 2,300-page, seven-novel cycle set in motion (and brought to closure) by a soggy cookie crumb, the definitive testimony to food's evocative, transporting power: a power greater than music, greater than photographs, greater than carefully stowed old clothes, maybe greater than anything. (Its only rival, smell, is taste's kissin' cousin.) I used to think that Proust just had a grotesque advantage over the rest of us, being French and all. I mean, lordylordylordy: *a decoction of lime flowers?* You go, Marcel. Me, I had to look up "decoction" in the dictionary. I'd context-guessed that it was sort of like "concoction," but really it means "an extract of flavor obtained by boiling." I'm pretty sure nobody in my family ever decocted anything, unless Jell-O counts.

My sister is a teacher. A real teacher, middle school, not a college professor like me. Late one night, I got a phone call from her. She had an uncharacteristic edge to her voice.

"What are our ethnic traditions?" She sounded like she was reading this. "What are the foods and customs that have shaped our family's heritage?"

"You sound like you're reading this," I said.

"I sort of am," she said. She teaches in a huge county school system in suburban Washington, DC, and she was taking a teacher-training in-service class, some state-mandated thing about ethnic sensitivity. "I have to give a presentation about this," she said.

The enormity of this was clear. We have no ethnicity. We grew up in a place as flavorless as the food we ate there and the times during which we ate it.

"You're screwed," I said. "Make stuff up."

"Exactly," she said. "Help me make stuff up."

This is what happens to you when you are the fiction writer in the family.

I can't remember what we made up. It was not inspired material, owing both to the lateness of the hour and also the dismal, unspoken realization that we look ineluctably like people who grew up where and how we did.

(Why, at least, didn't we think of the way food cemented the bond between *us?* While I was away at college, Shari started doing the cooking. Onions and garlic, basil and oregano all made their debuts in our house. "Chili" was actually replaced by chili [mild, but still]. "Casseroles" were replaced by actual food: lasagna! manicotti! ziti! [So what if Velveeta was involved? A corner had been turned.] That summer I was a lifeguard and a swimming-team coach at the public pool in the park across the street from my house. Swimming practice ended, the pool opened, and I didn't have time for lunch. Shari, one of the team's star swimmers, brought it to me. *Hot* lunches. She did not seem to mind, in fact seemed to enjoy, cooking that food and walking it over. I didn't mind driving her places. The four-year gap between us melted into inconsequence. That was the summer my sister and I became friends.)

Suddenly (I had been drinking) I came up with an idea. It's more or less what you've already read.

"Tell them about the soul food of our oppressed people!" I said. I was on a roll. "Learn it to the young'uns!"

"Have you been drinking?" she said.

"A little," I confessed.

"I'm serious," she said. "This presentation is next week."

(Right there you have it, the difference between us: I would have made a panicky call about a thing like this the night before it was due. Note to my students: I hate people like me.)

A week later, she got up in front of her class (she followed a middle-school art teacher whose mother was African American and whose father was a full-blooded Cherokee) and began with the line "I grew up in a house that never had an onion in it." People laughed like hell. No one believed her, she told me later. They thought they were laughing *with* her.

***

I am writing this on the first floor of a stone-and-stucco house at a place called Yaddo, in upstate New York. I've been here a month. Snow falls. It's about six o'clock on the night before the night before Christmas. Late tomorrow morning a taxi will come to pick me up and take me to the airport to fly home. (Soon after I get there, first my parents and then my sister and her family will arrive. For a week, then, our every move will be suffused with planning the next meal—as often as not, before the previous meal is even entirely eaten. One family tradition is for me to make a spitefully spicy chili, and my parents will find diplomatic ways to say they hate it; what no one knows is that this year I am, at thirty-six, finally mature enough to whip up a mild batch.) Home is now Tallahassee, Florida. Regional cuisine there is boiled peanuts and smoked mullet. Also fried gator tail. I've only lived there for a few months. None of this has taken.

(In truth, it hasn't taken with anybody. Boiled peanuts, smoked mullet, and fried gator tail are novelty cuisine, which, except in the state of Louisiana, is about all that's left of regional cuisine. In most of American nowhere—and America gets no more nowhere than Florida—regional cuisine and local custom have been franchised into nothingness, where every day is like TGIFriday's. In this respect, I—like many Ohioans—was born and raised so that I might grow up and move to live among the strip malls of Florida.)

At Yaddo *everything* revolves around food. The food here is plentiful and exquisite (last night, an amazing sea bass; tonight, I don't know, but I snuck by and was wowed silly—curry is involved), though the real blessing is the way food provides each day's productively self-indulgent structure.

All over this august, snow-draped place, in the various stone cottages and frame houses that dot the pine woods, writers write and painters paint and sculptors sculpt and composers compose and choreographers choreograph and filmmakers make films. (Occasionally people catnap.) This is nice. But here's what's important: The cook is cooking. I am not being glib. That's what's important: At six-thirty we will all convene for dinner.

You come to a place like this to work harder, with better focus and fewer distractions, than at home. But nothing—not even eradicating from your life the phone, or TV, or e-mail, or the quotidian errands that make up life *(brevis)* and kill art *(longa)*—matters more than the food. If I were home now, I'd stop writing. I've been working on this essay for a long time and I'm tired and I'd probably just start dinner (or more likely I would call my wife and then one of us would go to the store and forage, or else we'd go out, maybe to a franchised restaurant). But I *can't* start dinner. Dinner starts at six-thirty, today and every day. I have nothing to do between now and then but write.

Years from now I suspect that I will have to stop and think which hundred-page section of my next novel was written here. I won't be able to describe the splendidly dowdy-aunt interior of this room. I will not be able to remember what shirts I wore here. *Maybe*, if I am lucky, I will still be in touch with some of the friends I made here.

But for the rest of my life, whenever I taste sea bass, I'll be back here.

Whenever I see a black plastic lunch pail or a waxed-paper packet full of carrot sticks, I will think of these artists, trudging each snowy morning from the dining hall, where breakfast had just been served (I ate oatmeal every morning; I hadn't had oatmeal for twenty years), to their studios, a thermos of coffee in one hand, a winningly blue-collar black lunch pail in the other. Inside, the sandwiches and cookies vary. Some days there is couscous infused with golden raisins and grilled pine nuts. *Always* there are carrot sticks. Every day I happily ate them all, but I am sure that it will be a long time, after I eat the lunch I'll take with me on the plane tomorrow, before I eat another carrot stick.

I close my eyes. I swallow. I roll my tongue around in my mouth.

Carrot sticks. *Taste.*

Garlic-rubbed sea bass. *Taste.*

Whey-cheese lasagna. *Taste.*

Tuna fish stir-in "casserole." *Taste.*

Decoction of lime Jell-O. *Taste.*

Stale chili powder. *Taste.*

Brown the meat. *Taste.*

Raw (!) onion (!!) sprinkled over a fantasy of my most habañero-throttled chili. *Taste.*

Taste, *Smell. Take. Eat.*

about the author

MARK WINEGARDNER was born in Bryan, Ohio, home of the Dum-Dum Sucker and, in those days, the Etch A Sketch (since 2000, Ohio Art has been making them in Shenzhen, China). He graduated from Miami University (the first person in his family to finish college, though several male relatives had made it through the better part of their liquored-up freshmen years). His novel *Crooked River Burning* (Harcourt, 2001) received an award from *Cleveland Magazine* for being the definitive book about Cleveland. His nonfiction book *Prophet of the Sandlots* (Prentice Hall, 1990) is about the most successful baseball scout in history (Tony Lucadello, who happened to live in Fostoria, Ohio). Ohio is a frequent setting in his short story collection *That's True of Everybody* (Harcourt, 2002) and is the home of the narrator of his novel *The Veracruz Blues* (Viking, 1996).

Mario Puzo's editor and estate handpicked Winegardner to continue the Godfather saga, and Winegardner's novels *The Godfather Returns* (Random House, 2004) and *The Godfather's Revenge* (Putnam, 2006) each contain several scenes in Cleveland and at various points in and among the Erie Islands.

Winegardner is the Burroway Professor of English at Florida State University.

In Fields and Woods

Afternoons spent wandering among trees, knowing the shape of sycamore and sassafras, the shade of maple and oak. Summer days of splashing through creeks, digging under rocks, sliding in mud. The warmth of an egg just laid in the chicken coop; the pungent air of barns.

These were the Ohio childhoods of some remarkably talented writers. They grew up in the parts of the state where small towns gave way to county roads, woods, and pastures. Grown-ups left them alone to explore those worlds, sometimes in the company of siblings or cousins. These days, as we drive our children to team practices and build them playsets of sturdy plastic, such independence and such intimacy with the natural world seem dreamlike, the stuff of grainy home movies from another time.

It is, indeed, the Ohio of another era. The state is hardly immune from the scourge of suburbs and subdivisions felt across the country. Even when they aren't developed, those wild, vast playgrounds can change, as Elizabeth Dodd saw when a new owner turned her favorite woods of decades earlier into a hunting camp, and Scott Russell Sanders saw when the state flooded his beloved valley in Portage County to create a reservoir for recreation.

Mary Oliver, the Pulitzer Prize–winning poet, has lived for decades on Cape Cod, embracing salt air and sand dunes, but she still spends hours tromping through woods like she did as a kid in the then-pastoral Maple Heights. Likewise, philosopher and nature writer Kathleen Dean Moore, who grew up playing in creeks, continues to be drawn to rivers and the sea.

In one of her few media interviews, Oliver once talked of her childhood and her affinity with the natural world out her door. "The first way you take meaning from the physicality of the world, from your environment," she said, "probably never leaves you."

In Such a Homecoming

Elizabeth Dodd

ATHENS

Elizabeth Dodd, testing the waters with her mom

I can still understand my mother's dream of green quiet places and her struggle to reach them. And there were green places. As I think now of my own childhood, I can still feel an abrupt pang that rises not only from the shape of my parents' lives but also from the very disruption of the earth in Southeastern Ohio.

—James Wright

I WRITE THIS FAR, FAR FROM THE QUIET, green places in memory, the rumpled foothills of the Appalachian mountains and their accompanying plunging ravines, where height sloped steeply downward into creekbeds and hollows. It's nearly nine hundred miles, across the country's midsection, an asphalted journey through former landscapes—the transformed prairies and forests that once clothed the soil, under skies that dropped gradations of rainfall, moving toward the rainshadow cast by the Rockies' higher peaks. An academic itinerant, I moved west to Kansas to take the job that presented itself, and, as an adult, learned over several seasons to call tallgrass prairie home instead of hardwood forest. It's a sense of home I worked hard to build and, after a devastating divorce, to reinhabit on my own terms. During my marriage, I'd imagined the work I was doing to be making a kind of space for my ex-husband and me to share and flourish in; as the primary breadwinner for many years, I sometimes spoke of "making a clearing" for our lives together. I wanted to lay emotional claim to the territory I'd come to, and though I broke no literal ground, instead coming quickly to value the much-diminished expanse of indigenous grasslands that rippled under every wind, my metaphoric vocabulary drew on motifs of settlement. A friend once told me, "When you moved to Kansas, you really *moved to Kansas.*"

That's true, I like to think. I came into the country, and let it come into me. But it's also true that southeast Ohio remains fast in my psychological and emotional landscape, so that the whiff of fallen leaves in a hardwood forest, the damp touch of Ohio Valley humidity beneath my hair, along my neck—these are so deeply familiar, they suggest, indeed, the intimacy of family, of place-that-is-in-the-blood. But this kind of environmental legacy, this ecological intimacy, this sense of the land as *oikos*, home—it isn't a matter of simple residency, citizenship. It's a complexity, worth teasing apart, or trying to, to see whatever cause and pattern can be found.

～

"Where are *you* from?" It was the way children establish identities in the brief encounters that occur on family vacations. As the older sister, I answered for us both: my younger brother and me.

"We're from Ohio." A pause. Then, eliciting further conversation. "But ask us where we wish we lived."

The other child was obliging. "Okay. Where *do* you wish you lived?"

"Colorado. We used to live there, but we moved away when I was seven."

I remember this exchange, though I'm not sure where it took place: at the beach, at Nag's Head, maybe, the year we drove south and east to spend a week in an old-fashioned resort hotel, surely long since torn down for more aggressive development? Or were we actually on the road, perhaps gathered at a motel swimming pool, a Howard Johnson's maybe, somewhere along the interstate on the way west for one of the beloved summers spent, throughout my grade-school years, in the mountains of Colorado, the ostensible paradise we'd left behind?

Because, for some time, I adopted my mother's attitude towards our "new home" in southeast Ohio. She was desperately unhappy there, though it would take me years to realize that it was not *because* of Ohio, or even (which I also believed) because of *us*, her children. It was the nearly inexplicable fact that she had somehow taken up residence within the confines of deep, personality-crushing, even physically crippling depression, from which she couldn't emerge. And so our surroundings took on the dark colors of that psychological domesticity of despair, with its clouded windows and dusty staircase to the cold, closed-off second floor. The little hill town where we lived was "culturally deprived," the rivers and streams polluted, the countryside molested by decades of strip mining. I realize now, it was far too much like the worst aspects of eastern Oklahoma, the place of her childhood which she'd strived so hard to leave, investing heavily in education as a ticket up and out. So in her frustration, my mother took us to *West Virginia* ("oh, *Mother!*") to shop for school clothes, since there weren't adequate stores in town; as we drove south along Route 7, we passed coal-fired power plants, appalling in their inhuman belch and roar. And as we headed into the countryside for weekend visits to the various state parks, we'd pass tumbled-down coal tipples, unreclaimed mine sites, and creeks that ran oozing and crusted red or orange with acid mine drainage. Meanwhile, at school, my classmates (peers from Elsewhere, anyway), told West Virginia jokes, with Appalachia as the cultural butt end of every punch line.

But each summer, for a few brief years, our family drove back west and spent weeks in the mountains, in a primitive cabin resort where my mother boiled our drinking water, pumped up from the creek in a thick black hose; where we had fires in the fireplace even in July; where one morning I awoke and, looking straight out from the cabin's porch, saw fresh snow topping the peak in the distance. In reality, this too, was a ravaged country: the immediate area had been a nineteenth-century mining center, and on a long walk we sometimes took up the canyon, we'd come across tipples and shafts and pale, sulfurous slag heaps from the boom and bust days of the gold mines. But it was paradise. My parents fly-fished, my father spent the mornings writing, and my brother and I wandered the aspen-rustling hillsides, learned to read where avalanches had bent or broken the slender trees, visited the astonishing communes of anthills, conglomerates of pine needles and grains of granite. Once, I recall, we found one torn apart by digging: a bear, most likely, and we hurried back to tell about it.

It was, I'm sure, this migrant lifestyle that delayed my own identification with Ohio as home, reinforced by my mother's bitter unhappiness in our hillside house on Grosvenor Street, her disgust with the junky used-car lot down the street, the local, unfamiliar accent that said "spatial" when people really meant "special." What was it, finally, that changed my mind? That is, what changed *me* and the myriad subtle, even subliminal emotional whispers that would shift from "there" to "here"?

It's a complicated process, the way in which we learn about our place in the world. I don't mean by this primarily one's social position—class, or caste, one's ranking in the pecking order that is the economic reality in which a family, figuratively, resides. I mean really, literally, the *place* itself: the lay of the land, the rhythm of its weathers, the precessional change that the seasons bring throughout the year, the march of shadows, drought, and frost across the enduring ground. We all know the fact of Americans' mobility: from a history of immigration, we have settled into an expectation of transience, moving on average every five years or so. Some of this movement is from the apartment or starter home into a larger house, the upward mobility of real-estate acquisition. Some of it is due to the severance of divorce, the rupture and fission of households. But much of it is, indeed, a kind of itinerancy, following a job, or a company relocation. That's how we came to Ohio, following my father's career. We joined a university community already seething with the conflict over the Vietnam War. Throughout my time in the public schools, hostility was bristly and virulent between children of local families who'd lived in the area for generations, and children of newcomers, whose parents most likely worked for the university. There remained a shadow of colonialism; Appalachia had long been a place removed from the sources of power; it was a land that supplied resources through extractive industry (timber, iron, coal) with very little development of locally controlled wealth. So it was true from the outset, we were outsiders.

The disintegration of my parents' marriage, my mother's moving out of the house—our house—while my brother and I remained with our father; this, of course, figured largely in our emotional lives. It was unusual: my father became the custodial parent, deeply, unceasingly dedicated to the role. For a few years, we remained in the bedrooms where we'd chosen the wallpaper, in the house from which we could *all* walk to school—my brother to East Elementary, me to Athens Middle School, my father to the university campus. We no longer hired the woman from out in the county to come clean house. Instead, a weekly list of chores hung on the refrigerator, and my brother and I were to initial each job as we completed it, choosing and owning the work we did for the household. In those few years, as if in a perplexing modernist novel chapter called, say, "Time Passes," further change unfolded before and around us, which can be elided into the barest of narrative summary: I entered high school; we moved several miles out of town, to the country; my father remarried. But I want to examine what happened when and how I stepped out of the confines that my mother's despair had erected like heavy Victorian drapes. Long before my first semester in the university dorm, or my first apartment, I spent increasing time out of the house, *outside*, in the second- and third-growth forests that had reclaimed southern Ohio from the nineteenth-century attempts at subsistence agriculture on steep, clay slopes. One year I was given a tent; another, cross-country skis. I remember heading to the woods, to a particular tree I considered a good location for thought, to write a paper for my high-school English class. In college, I took a sociology course that focused on Appalachia. I read Harry Caudill's *Night Comes to the Cumberlands* and learned, with surprise, of indentured servitude's role in the settlement of the region. I learned of Zane's Trace and the Northwest Territory; I read about Simon Kenton in historical novels by Allan W. Eckert, and I read James Wright's poetry precociously and naively. But I believe it was the time spent outdoors, in contact with land itself, that suggested to me I was not ultimately, irrevocably, an alienated outsider.

Once my father and stepmother moved out to the county, my brother and I had miles and miles to explore. We rode our bicycles five curving miles, the last three all downhill, to the state park at Dow Lake, and then turned around for the slow, low-gear grind back up, with each bend in the blacktop road marked by the scent of its foliage: oak leaf, sumac, sycamore. A distance runner, I'd sometimes jog the route as well, returning home elated with exhaustion. On foot, together we wandered into each steep ravine, and, hike by hike, we came across the history of settlement along the watersheds of Peach Ridge. In one hillside pocket, we found the sandstone foundations of a house long since melted away, and, a few hundred yards below, a spot where someone once had set a great ceramic crock, with a hole knocked in its bottom, into the hillside. A slow seep of a spring would have once gathered there in a kind of well, but by then the crock was filled with dirt. I imagined the family living there, perhaps daily drawing this "well-water" faster than the seep could refill the crock; perhaps, I reasoned, they had a rain barrel, too? We came back with shovels and wrestled the artifact up, out of the clutch of hillside clay. It must have taken us most of an afternoon; it took muscle-knotting effort, and I loved it. The deeper we dug, the sloppier the soil; we knelt in the mud, sat in the mud, pulled mud from within the cavity and around its base. Finally, muddily triumphant, we rolled it uphill to the ridgetop road, and on along the quarter mile to home. My stepmother recognized its worth instantly, and with a flourish of enthusiasm made it a planter, to keep things alive and blooming near the house.

One winter day, layered in long johns and boots, my brother and I headed miles away, along a deeply cut ravine that met up with another such side valley and then opened into a tiny flat spot with the narrow trace of a stream flowing past, just enough level land for two log cabins that still stood there, rotting darkly among the piebald sycamores. From the much-collapsed doorway of one, I stood still and looked straight up, imagining how the hills, day after day, would allow only a segment of sunlight past their steep, austere horizons. Sunlight maybe from ten to three, as in the song about Kentucky's deep valleys and the darkness of poverty. Even farther down that same trickle of stream we found a house of frame construction, with newsprint from the 1940s papering the walls. Beavers had dammed the creek and built their stick-mound of a lodge, and we spent time pond-side, then and later, hoping for a glimpse of the animals themselves. I knew that formerly, the animals had almost disappeared from many American waterway systems, trapped into scarcity for their pelts; it seemed marvelous to know they'd come back here, to homestead where the people had given up and moved out.

Even farther down that hollow the valley widened, opening into a tiny rural community, an actual store (long since abandoned, of course), with an old tin roof and a rusted sign leaning against the wall. It was summer when we found it: the place was lush and dense with the spider webs that lace together the underbrush, and clotted with the great snarls of greenbrier that take over disturbed land, leaving decades-long legacies of thorn and thicket. The air must have smelled like sassafras, a scent I think of now in nostalgic absence, half a continent away. A house and a barn stood nearby, all dating to perhaps the first few decades of the twentieth century. Exploring among the fallen boards, the rusting machinery, the summer-warmed undergrowth of jewelweed and bracken, we startled a large snake which startled us even more. A copperhead! My brother, urging me to stand back, killed it. And so we'd had a kind of testing far from home, it felt to us then; we had journeyed in, and come through danger, and made our way back safely to tell the tale.

These were the woods adventures of my adolescence and my brother's childhood; they allowed us to step right out the front door into a kind of historic frontier, where we examined the hillsides for bits of history: hidden pathways of old roads, former homesteads, the current communities of maturing hardwood. It's easy to see these as the archetypal enactments they were, and even at the time I knew how performative of inner discoveries our travels were (I was, after all, a reader and writer, even then). When we told the story of the slain snake, I am sure I smiled at the symbolism of it: my brother, deep in the forest, had dispatched the dragon that lived among the ruins and had saved his sister's life. The fact that neither of us was ever in any real danger made the death of the snake unnecessary, but, an isolated event, it didn't mark my brother as an habitual or senseless killer, not by a long shot. It was mythic imagination, playing out in the landscape where we were growing to maturity, marking us and changing us in the period of our lives that's evolutionarily dedicated to change.

This kind of play is today almost absent from American childhoods: there are soccer leagues and expansive, halogen-lit playing fields; there is concern about predatory adults who may molest or kidnap or kill; and there's less and less land left fallow amidst development. Today, the valley where we found the abandoned store and killed the snake is a small, upscale subdivision, planted with fescue in among the thinned trees, with signs declaring, in lettering that looks well paid for, Private Drive. The hillside where we excavated the crock lies just across the road from a large parcel of land owned privately by out-of-towners as a hunting zone. One recent year, as adults coming back to visit, we scorned the braying red-and-black perimeter of tacked-up NO TRESPASSING signs, and trudged, silent and grim, along bush-hogged pathways to the specter of feeding stations, where plastic barrels of corn lay in wait for later, deadly use beneath the shooting platforms riveted into the trees. Though it wasn't yet rifle season (the very reason why we dared to climb over the metal gate that blocked entrance, and head into those woods), we could easily picture the men in camouflage, coiled above the bait, waiting. The landscape was in the grip of killers, wealthy and, we felt certain, walking home along the low-grade black-top, unprincipled.

I'm certainly not the only person who believes that getting outside helps the mind believe in its own good health. The writer Richard Louv openly discusses a nature-deficit disorder which he believes afflicts American children, often in the form of ADHD. But it wasn't just play in the acres and miles that lay in concentric fields of walking distance around our house in the southeast Ohio woods that, I believe, allowed us to "come home" to Ohio in our psyches. One spring break, I took my brother camping in Zaleski State Forest. I think it was the first or second year I owned a car, an ancient black VW Bug, as old as I was, anyway, hardly highway safe, but I drove it around the southern part of the state, hoping not to get stopped for any inspection, since the turn signal didn't work. Neither did the horn, come to think of it, and on the passenger side there were holes in the floor large enough to catch glimpses of road rushing beneath. But the car ran, and it was mine, and together he and I piled our gear in the back and drove to a trailhead in hardwood forest for a weekend backpacking trip. It was too early for most wildflowers—trillium and spring beauty would bloom soon, but not yet—and we nearly froze overnight, but despite its spartan minimalism, I think of that trip as the inauguration of decades, later, of camping together.

Another time, I signed us up for a century ride, an organized cycling trip to Forked Run State Park, beside the Ohio River. Our entry fee secured room for our gear in the "sag wagon" and paid for two meals, dinner that night and breakfast the next morning. It was the longest ride either of us had ever made; I was nineteen or twenty, my brother thirteen or fourteen, before he underwent the transformational growth that would, forever after, reverse our roles and leave me following in his athletic wake, trying to keep up. We hung together for much of the ride; though, in the social throng of pedalers, we'd sometimes go separate ways and travel in conversation with some other acquaintance. Two of the riders had been our next-door neighbors when we lived in town, owners of a bicycle and outdoors store. Another couple were current neighbors from the country who lived across the hollow. The year before, they'd taught me how to ski cross-country, crashing ungainly but elated along forest trails they'd cleared near their place.

We pedaled fifty miles that day, over back roads heading south and east; for a brief, alert while we strung out along a state highway but then turned off again, into more quiet miles among trees. The park itself sprawls over a couple of thousand acres, where the Shade River joins the Ohio. It's bottomland: wet and warm and buggy, the air thick with the river's respiration, as well as the trees'; and, of course, our own hot panting as we rolled slowly in and leaned the bikes against a sapling. We pitched our tent—my first tent, I realize; it must have been fairly new then—and I lay down to fall instantly asleep. My little brother, a skinny, smooth-faced boy already developing greater stamina, went swimming in a pond and later stood in line for our dinner and brought mine back to me, where I lay crushed by exertion. That evening the campground was dotted with wood fires and low voices, interrupted occasionally by the percussion of someone's laughter. And the next morning, after a terrifically caloric breakfast, our gear stashed in the support van, we headed back up north, fifty miles again, into the hills of our home county.

One year I spent a weekend backpacking with my college roommate, another local girl who'd stayed close to go to school in our hometown. In high school, she and I had hiked together in England's Lake District, forever cold and wet, hoping each night at the youth hostel to dry our perpetually sodden gear. I was near-hypothermic the entire time I tramped through Wordsworth's country, and she developed the worst set of blisters I've ever seen and would lance them in the evening, in whatever castle or tower-turned-hostel we'd reached for the night, while I watched with horrified interest. Once, we had sat together in the evening's gathering chill beside Loch Ness, wondering what would happen if we actually glimpsed anything unusual out across the water, in the misty distance. We'd crossed Mount Helvellyn's scree-field crust and descended to a little village pub where I ate steak-and-kidney pie and thought it was the most deliciously hot meal possible: Pangloss potpie. So here we chose a sunny, warm weekend in autumn. With the hillsides nearly leafless, we moved through extravagant sunlight in southeast Ohio's hilly terrain.

The trail meandered through handsome stands of hardwood, curving in and out of hollows and ravines, but also crossed through pine plantations that had replaced some former clearcut. We carried all our water for the weekend; my friend's father, a biologist at the university, studied the effects of acid mine drainage on the invertebrate population, and we considered ourselves forewarned. We had no intention of drinking any water we came across, in coal-mining country. At one point the trail crossed a wasteland of tailings: it was hardpan, with hardly any vegetation at all. Water pooled in red and orange, oozy-looking shallows. Wounds, obviously. Unhealed and leaking.

But the trail moved back into forest, and we followed its horizontal saunter across a history of land use: former farms, former roads, sections of variously aged forest. We came upon two young men, tents pitched behind them while they sprawled in the sunlight, eating from an aluminum pot of macaroni and cheese the color of mine drainage. We passed rock outcrops and overhangs, cloaked in thick moss and trailing the litter of fallen leaves—season after season of accumulation, from the forest's dropped canopy. We ate peanut butter and apple and chocolate. We talked almost incessantly, as young women often do, exploring and airing our feelings, our thoughts, the inner lives which, at that point, had much in common. And that night we pitched our tent—my tent— alone in the margin of light before dusk, and cooked the utterly unimaginative meal of ramen noodles over her brand-new, exquisitely minimalist backpacking stove. It wasn't wilderness, but it was, then, lovely: dark skies above the near-bare branches.

And so, in the contemplation of how I learned to feel at home in southeast Ohio, I've stepped into the pathway of memoir, holding memory's imperfect thumbprint images of a quarter-century ago, when, emerging first into and then from adolescence, I moved across the Appalachian landscape, *a place*, as we say tiredly of those whose lives have taken more than one questionable turn, *with a past*. Somehow the patterns left by earlier eras seemed to me, most often, poignant: the great coke furnace named, as if in purposeful irony, the Hope Furnace, where slag still lies in cast-off piles from the years when old-growth hardwood was turned to charcoal to fuel the iron mills that, for example, made most of the cannonballs for the Civil War. Or the occasional depressions in the forest recognizable as old cellarholes; sometimes, even in the depth of the returned forest, daffodils still bloom in banks that mark a former walkway, or the spot beneath a window where a woman must have looked outside to see their color, early utterances of spring.

~

When, a year ago, I had the opportunity to make a kind of pilgrimage to a tiny stand of tallgrass prairie back in the upland forest country of southeast Ohio, the possibility instantly rose up tinted with the shadows and gilt trim of symbolism. Could this be a kind of circling back, a chance to put worlds together—"my" worlds, that is, of forest and prairie, past and present? It was a chance to come outside again, in the middle of my adulthood, and explore the world of my childhood—the *world* itself, not just my narrative footpath through the realm of memory. In such a homecoming, I'd be again on the land, in my skin, coming into the country of the self through the sensory play of place upon person.

Buffalo Beats is a tiny open spot in the hardwood forest, less than an acre of grass and forbs beneath—on that particular day—a dinner platter of blue sky, clear and full of October light. I'd read about this place years before, and marveled at it: such a minuscule portion of prairie, a relict of what has been called the prairie peninsula, the fingers of grassland that, presumably during warmer, drier cycles in the climate of the distant past, reached this eastern-most position in Ohio. It's amusing, and rather touching, to read the early descriptions of the place in scientific publications. In the mid-1940s, a researcher wrote of "the date of migration and the migration routes of the ancestors of the prairie plants" of such isolated grasslands. Were these personifications invasions from the west, dating to some time before the great glaciation periods, the Illinoisan and Wisconsinian? Or were they later arrivals, come up from Kentucky, like the many rural Appalachians who, mid-twentieth century, left the green hollows for work in Ohio cities? And so, from a distance, across the smooth margin of the desk and the page, I took it as a personal symbol, a kind of mental amulet I carried in imagination instead of on my person.

This prairie relict is a secret place, defined in part by its fragility, not open to the public though it lies on public land, and it takes some work to parlay my way there. But on the day I'm scheduled to visit, I arrive to find that my contact has called in sick, and so another Forest Service employee kindly agrees to make time in her day to take me there. She's not a botanist and she hasn't been to the site very often, but she seems cheerful about the task. After all, it's a beautiful day, and she's glad to put on her boots and head into the field. We drive a few miles along dirt back roads and leave my car, with the fine dust of Kansas still clinging to its hubcaps, to explore the hillside. She's not sure precisely where it is, so we must canvass the area; from a high point, I scan the forest with my binoculars, looking for some pattern of light and shadow, or the pale hint of grass in sunlight. Patterns: I think one must always look for patterns, possible shapes of meaning in the apparent world.

And it works; I pass her the field glasses, and we agree, *that* looks like an opening in the forest, on a hill in the near distance. We move through the mild autumn day and step into the clearing; the sunlight catches in the drying grass and looks nearly ethereal. Today, I can recognize many of these plants, though I wouldn't have growing up: big bluestem, Indian grass, New Jersey tea, prairie gayfeather. The latter, *liatris*, now grows in my front yard, beside the mailbox. Yet here we stand, in Ohio, in the crisp, sun-warmed smell of hardwood forest, the deciduous whiff of one home, and the dry-stemmed glint and wind-whisper of another. How powerfully smell figures in memory, in emotion, in what we call in animals *territoriality*, the endocrine system laying synaptic and hormonal claim to the world that impinges on us richly, through the portals of our senses.

There was once a footpath that ran here between the little communities of Happy Valley and Utah Ridge to the town of Buchtel; we can see no trace of it among the grasses, though it can, on occasion, be found in the surrounding woods. It dates to a time when people would have walked, often, from home to town, or elsewhere in the cycles of their daily business; I think of the various tiny communities—a house or two, or the place I've inwardly named the Store in Snake Hollow—which my brother and I rediscovered in our cozy adventures, fanning out from home, and the possible paths we must have retraced along ridge and ravine. Today, arriving at the opening in the forest, we're ringed by hardwoods, living palings that demark the encroaching perimeter of the trees. I stand in the center of the circle of grass and turn slowly, looking up, looking all around. I sit down, grass reaching just over my head, and the forest disappears. I stand again, and the prairie instantly shrinks, domesticated by vertical perspective.

This little holdout of tallgrass has, indeed, held on. Researchers say the soil record suggests a grassland community existed here at least some thirteen thousand years ago. It's a tiny portion of the Pleistocene world, a bit of grassland once grazed and ranged by the vanished animals that lived south of the ice sheet: the giant ground sloth, stag moose, musk ox, mammoth and mastodon, and perhaps, in some nearby lowland swamp, the preposterously giant beaver the size of a bear, called *Castoroides ohioensis*. I like the possibility of these distant beaver kin existing somewhere close by; I like the fact that the first remains of a *Castoroides* lodge ever found was also in Ohio, along the Beaver River in the western part of the state. I think of the beaver lodge my brother and I found along the little creek two ravines away from home; I think as well of the beaver dam that broke, one summer, on the Colorado stream we lived along, and how the resultant flood amazed us with its force and stagnant smell. And in the flood of memory, of worlds converging within me as well as without, I stand still in this, the middle of my life, and see again my little brother in his blue-striped shirt, standing beside me, or already moving off ahead.

about the author

Born in Colorado, ELIZABETH DODD grew up in southeast Ohio and has lived in the tallgrass prairie region of Kansas for more than a decade and a half. An English professor and director of the creative writing program at Kansas State University, Dodd has written two books of poetry—*Like Memory, Caverns* (New York University Press, 1992) and *Archetypal Light* (University of Nevada Press, 2001); a book of criticism, *The Veiled Mirror and the Woman Poet* (University of Missouri Press, 1992); and most recently a collection of nonfiction essays, *Prospect: Journeys & Landscapes* (University of Utah Press, 2003), winner of the William Nelson Rockhill Award for nonfiction. She is a contributing editor to *Tar River Poetry* and an editorial advisory board member for *ISLE: Interdisciplinary Studies in Literature and Environment*.

We Are Mapmakers

Anthony Doerr

NOVELTY

Tony Doerr in his Novelty backyard

WE ARE IN NOVELTY FOR THANKSGIVING.

Six days, seven inches of snow, 20 degrees. Everything is familiar and new all at once: the slickness of well water in the shower, as if I can never rinse off all the soap; the leafless hardwoods ringing my parents' house; the smells of slush, gasoline, and wood in the garage. Out the windows everything is either gray or white. The radio burbles out another storm warning; my mother's three Muscovy ducks march single-file (Siegfried, then Roy, then Elvis) across the backyard, plowing a track through the snow. Our not-quite-two-year-old sons take toothpicks out of a kitchen drawer and transport them one by one across the family room and drop them into the heating register.

I have not been to Novelty in almost two years. I have not lived here in a decade. But to return to where I grew up, these six acres beside a pond, is to wander through a thicket of memories. My feet know which paths to take through the snow; my hands find the two hollows in the sycamore beside the beach where I used to do pull-ups.

Over there is the swamp, which I once came staggering out of, black with mud, while my brother filmed me with a Betamax camcorder. Over there I drove my dad's GMC off the road and wedged it between two trees. There we played a thousand tackle football games; there in a church, that's no longer standing, I was eight years old and in love with a blonde girl whom I never met, whose family always sat in the front. I used to wrap my hands around the back of the pew and look from the girl to the backs of my hands to the backs of my brothers' hands, wondering about family, about heredity.

We are mapmakers, all of us, tracing lines of memory across the spaces we enter. We embed memories everywhere; we inscribe a private and complicated diagram across the landscape; we plant root structures of smells and textures in the apartments of girlfriends and the station wagons of friends and in the living rooms of our parents. Viewed from above, our memories might look like a satellite photo of Earth at night: a black half-sphere punctuated here and there by clusters of lights.

There are the population centers, the known territories, the illuminated districts. We live in them; we feel (mostly) safe; we layer memories atop memories.

Elsewhere the lights make slender ramifications into the dark, a few threads of flame burning here and there, five months in Kenya, a winter in New Zealand, a year in Rome.

And then there are the uncharted realms, the encircling oceans of shadow, the borderlands, unsurveyed and unknown. Our Antarcticas, our Neptunes.

On my own map of the world, my parents' kitchen window in Novelty is perhaps the brightest light; it is the capitol building in the capital city, with a broad staircase and long views down an avenue studded with lanterns. I look through the glass into the backyard, and every tree, every post of my mother's garden fence, is a candle to a memory, and each of those memories, as it rises out of the ground, is linked to a dozen more.

I used to stand on those same patio chairs to reach tools in the garage; I used to throw a football onto the section of the roof above this window and wait for it to come rolling off the gutter. I used to follow deer tracks through that section of woods just beyond the burn pile. I shot a squirrel out of that locust tree and carried its body on the blade of a shovel to the compost pile. I planted that magnolia. I made tie-dyed T-shirts one summer day in the same spot where my sons' little bootprints now crisscross the snow, and I climbed that crumbling skeleton of an oak and helped Dad hang the bird feeder that dangles now above a spray of sunflower seeds, black against the white.

Whole scaffoldings of memory rise from the snow, cantilevering themselves out into space. My grandmother stood straight-backed one afternoon peering out this same window into a thunderstorm. Her hands were clamped around the handles of her purse. Lightning strobed the trees.

"Boy, look at all the leaves," she said. She was often commenting on the quantity of leaves in the backyard. Clots of rain shelled the deck and curtains of rainwater swung from the gutters. The power went out. I remember watching with her, both of us quiet, the afternoon turned to dusk, the leaves flashing their undersides.

Other days she peered out this window at my dad as he mowed the lawn, or the birds bolting down seeds at the feeder. She'd say things like, "Do they have iced tea at this place?" or, more frequently, "Do you think someone around here will be able to take me home?"

"You *are* home, Grandma," I'd say. "You live here now." But at night she'd stand in the hall and call the names of my parents into the dark.

I returned to Novelty in April of 2001, when Grandma was about to die. She had long since moved into an Alzheimer's center, and I stood at this same kitchen window before driving to Chardon to sit with her in her room. Classical music played on her bedside radio. She had a wooden dresser imprinted with a maple leaf, whose twin stood in my bedroom. Out in the hall, I remember, a patient was screaming, the kind of scream that, in another context, means someone has lost a family member.

Grandma was asleep. Her breath rasped in and out. Her hair was mostly gone and her dentures were out, so that her lips were caved in and slightly open, and she looked as if she, too, were screaming. I remember thinking that her skin had gradually thinned over the years, until now it seemed hardly a barrier at all.

Each time her breath changed, or her cheek flexed, I'd sweat a little, afraid something bad was happening, afraid I'd be the one to have to deal with it. By then Grandma's memories were entirely inaccessible, warped beneath plaques, lost in neurofibrillary tangles, and she was my mother's mother in name only. A person dies, or loses her memory, and her map of the world plunges into darkness forever. She died a day later.

Every hour, all over the globe, an infinite number of memories disappear, whole glowing atlases dragged into graves. But during that same hour children are moving about, surveying territory that seems to them entirely new. They push back the darkness; they scatter memories behind them like breadcrumbs. Lines sharpen, contours deepen. The world is remade.

In six days at my parents' house my sons have learned how to say, "rocks," "heavy," and "snowman." They've learned the names of their cousins, and the smell of the chicken coop, and each one took, for the first time in his life, a warm brown egg out of a laying box and carried it in his hand through the backyard snow.

On a map in their room, when we get home, we'll put a sticker over northeast Ohio that reads, "I've been here." My grandmother's map of Novelty is long gone, but my sons are just starting on theirs.

We return to the places we're from; we trample faded corners and pencil in new lines. "They grow up so fast," seemingly everyone tells us, gesturing at our children. But they're wrong. You bury your childhood everywhere you go. It waits for you, all your life, to come and dig it back up.

By late afternoon the snow has stopped. My father stuffs a big, pink turkey with scraps of bread and sausage. Out the window the clouds shift and sunlight avalanches across the yard. The shadows of trees lunge across the pond. The snow seems about to incandesce. You forget that sunlight can be so pure, pouring through the windows, splashing across the kitchen. It brings tears to your eyes.

Henry, my son, carries a toothpick past me into the living room and sets it on the lid of my mother's piano. "Hap-py," he says, and looks up at me.

about the author

ANTHONY DOERR's first book, *The Shell Collector* (Scribner, 2002), a volume of eight stories, won the Barnes and Noble Discover Prize, two O. Henry Prizes, the Rome Prize, and the Ohioana Book Award. He followed with a first novel, *About Grace* (Scribner, 2004), which was named one of the five best books of 2004. His fiction has appeared in numerous publications, including *The O. Henry Prize Stories*, the *Paris Review*, the *Atlantic Monthly*, *Zoetrope: All Story*, and *The Best American Short Stories*. He also reviews science-related books for the *Boston Globe*.

After growing up in northeast Ohio, Doerr graduated from Bowdoin College in Maine. He has lived in Africa, New Zealand, and Rome. He lives now with his wife and two sons in Boise, Idaho.

The Mere Breath of Sheep

Andrea Louie

WAYNE COUNTY

Andrea Louie with her dog, Zea, and mother on their Wayne County farm

"I USED TO CASTRATE SHEEP." I TOLD THIS story whenever I wanted to make men uncomfortable, usually at some large gathering where I was bored or annoyed or both. Now I'm mortified by my petty tactics, ashamed to admit how much pleasure I found in that delicious, horrified pause—an instant before, simultaneously, the men's faces collapsed into a wince.

Yet looking back, it astonishes me how willing I was to pawn my history for a cocktail-party witticism, trading in some of my most private misgivings to buy a five-second laugh.

I grew up in rural Ohio, a landscape that embodied the very best of America. Owning a little place in the country like this is such a romantic notion; we long for an uncomplicated life. But nothing is ever simple, and during the years my family lived on a farm in Wayne County, we were so close to the earth I thought it would swallow us whole.

Before my parents bought the farm, we lived on an L-shaped suburban street in Wooster, a small college town an hour south of Cleveland. Wooster was the home of Rubbermaid; nearby is the Smucker's jam factory. Most of the grown-ups I knew worked on assembly lines or as secretaries. My classmate's father was a butcher at the downtown Buehler's supermarket. Every year at auction, Buehler's bought the grand-champion steer from the Wayne County Fair; they prominently displayed the purple velvet prize banner over the beef counter, suggesting—improbably— that every Styrofoam package had originated from that once-cherished specimen.

On Linwood Drive there were kids and bicycles and shiny pieces of lawn equipment. Our pale yellow ranch-style house was situated on more than an acre of land, a corner lot bordered by a creek on one side and a dozen white pines on the other. I was in between the ages of the other children, so I didn't play with them, instead spending hours on an upholstered rocking chair in the living room, reading one library book after another. My mother and I were housebound when my father was at work; there was no public transportation, and we were a fifteen-minute drive away from the nearest store of any sort. Linwood Drive was on the outskirts of town, and the tract homes soon gave way to dairy farms and acres of corn and wheat and potatoes.

My father was a specialist in corn diseases at an agricultural research-and-development center, which only partly explained our exile in Wayne

County. My parents had moved to Ohio not only because of my father's work but also because of a nearly migratory desire for escape—from West Coast families and their ongoing sibling brawls, from lingering resentments and shallowly buried sadness. For my parents, the great expanse of Middle America was exquisitely flat, bland, and banal; this was a landscape without memory. As newlyweds in 1962, my parents bundled their meager possessions into a Volkswagen Beetle and headed east from San Francisco to Ithaca, New York, where my father attended graduate school. (This cross-country drive was their honeymoon, and they meant to stop at the Grand Canyon but missed it because my mother is not good with maps.) They drove through Ohio, marveling at how beautiful it was. When my father finished his doctorate, two job opportunities presented themselves: one in Mississippi and the other in Wayne County, Ohio. They packed up the Beetle again, this time with me, a two-year-old, strapped into the back seat and peering out from beneath a white cloth cap.

It was 1968, and there were two other Asian American families in the area. Mr. Yamazaki was a professor at the College of Wooster; the Lee family ran a hand laundry downtown. Although we ran into each other from time to time and were pleasant in that midwestern way, our families did not associate. My parents kept to themselves, and I had one girlfriend whom I saw only at school. We didn't belong to a church or play bingo or sign up for softball in the park. I was not permitted to join Girl Scouts because my parents mistrusted any organization that gave badges for accomplishing tasks that should have been done anyway. This was the land of potluck suppers and neighborhood barbeques, yet we remained suspended contentedly in our own private sphere, our relations more than half a continent away.

My parents are not unusually high-spirited people nor terribly adventurous, but neither did they want to lose their decades in slow increments, one situation comedy and a carton of milk at a time. They didn't want to farm, but they decided they wanted to take care of something, a small act of defiance against routine and inertia. After two years of searching, they found a piece of property they liked, and we moved across town just after my sophomore year in high school. The farm was eighty-two acres in Green Township, a rectangle of rich Wayne County soil a half-mile long and a quarter wide. The property dipped in the middle, as though into the spine of an open book. A narrow creek ran through this valley, hidden year round by a thicket of brambles and grass; yet one could always hear the merry sound of water in the distance, leading to a tiny pond clotted with algae. Most of the acreage was rented by a neighboring farmer who planted field corn and alfalfa in alternating years.

The farm particularly suited my father, who is good with his hands and delights in anything resembling a puzzle. He can lure clocks that have been stalled for decades into motion and has a knack for resuscitating any piece of forsaken machinery. In the basement of our Linwood Drive house he had fashioned two dining tables and a kitchen island for my mother. He sent away for special kits and taught himself first how to pick locks and then how to sew an entire down parka, which he wore for years.

My father got the sheep primarily as a tax write-off, something to do with pretending we actually operated a working farm. He quickly exhausted himself by trying to do everything without hiring outside help to save money—all while keeping his full-time research job. Using only a hammer and crowbar, we helped him dismantle an entire abandoned old house that stood on the property; the salvaged wood was made into fencing for inside the barn. We enclosed much of the surrounding pasture area with an electric fence, digging postholes with the aid of a tractor attachment and prying out stones with a shovel. He disemboweled an old washing machine, removed the motor, and turned it into a contraption for shelling dried field corn. My mother and I planted, weeded, and harvested a whole acre of field corn by hand, trudging up and down the long rows in the hot sun wearing old tennis hats—though none of us had ever played tennis.

My mother argued with my father constantly, saying he was trying to do too much and would drive us all crazy with his constant demands and ill temper. My father wouldn't listen, and after a while my mother gave up. She kept quiet and developed a chronic bleeding ulcer instead. I became sullen and resented my father's exacting specifications on how each chore should be performed, from painting to mowing the lawn. By the time the sheep were purchased and unloaded into the newly fenced pastures, we were all irritable and overwhelmed. But we were in for the long haul, and there was nothing to do but keep going. We realized we knew nothing of animal husbandry outside of having a dog for a pet. For the rest, my father had to resort to books ordered from the United States Agricultural Extension Service.

This was more or less how we learned to castrate sheep. We went out to the barn in the pale cold of winter, our movements awkward and humorous in our thick, padded clothes. Our hands were bare. I sat in a chair with a tiny lamb, usually not more than three or four weeks old, between my knees. We did them this young because the nerve endings and blood vessels have not yet fully developed, hopefully making the procedure easier on all concerned. I sat up the lamb and held his knobby legs in my hands, and my father, in as swift a motion as he could muster, sliced through half the woolly scrotum with a razor blade. The lamb let out a heartbreaking bleat, throwing his little head into my chest. Behind us, the ewes began screaming. My father reached into the small genital sack and pulled out two slippery nodules, which were attached with alarming tenacity. The lambs all bleated, and the ewes kept screaming; behind us, the animals darted frantically in their pens, rushing from one end to another. I talked gently to the lamb throughout the entire procedure—silly, pointless blather about how this all would soon be over, there there, we were almost done now.

My mother stood by with a cardboard canister of something called, no kidding, Blood Stopper. Afterward, my father sprinkled this on liberally, like so much parmesan cheese. And with a stiff rub and a pat, I gently lifted the lamb and set him down, wobbling, back into the pen.

At our height, we had thirty lambs every winter, which meant that we did around a dozen castrations every January. That was nothing for a real farmer, but we were gentleman farmers with just a mongrel dog, a bored ram, thirteen shrill ewes, and only a faint idea of what we were doing.

During the deep chill of January, the downstairs pen in the barn was warm, the air moist with the sweet breath of sheep and rusty with the smell of new blood and birth. The sheep shuffled and stamped their feet in the straw, the hissing stream of their piss penetrating the earthen ground. The sheep were very quiet when alone, but as soon as one of us turned on the light, they all leaped to their feet in anticipation. During lambing season, we fed the mothers twice a day, with shelled field corn and pats of hay thrown into bins. We chiseled out the ice from plastic five-gallon buckets and put down fresh straw. Before midnight, we ventured in for one last look, checking for new arrivals.

You can usually tell when a ewe is ready to lamb. She drifts off by herself, pawing at the ground with her front hooves and turning in one circle after another in some ancient, primal ritual. She may not eat. If all goes well, the birth of a lamb is a beautifully uncomplicated process. A ewe stands off by herself, bears down, and the slick casing of the lamb slips out with shocking efficiency. The ewe turns around and licks the placenta off the lamb's mouth and nose; then she works her way over the rest of the compact, wet body, at once drying the lamb and stimulating its circulation. Then, barely ten minutes after the birth, the ewe nudges the tiny lamb to its feet. Within twenty minutes, the lamb is usually teetering around, latching on to its mother's teats with ferocious nips. In the wild, a lamb that is not on its feet is a marked one, spotted by wolves and coyotes lingering at the periphery of herds, smelling blood and vulnerability.

Sometimes, in multiple births, a ewe will be seized with contractions to deliver the second or third lamb before she has a chance to lick clean the nostrils of her newly birthed baby, and the lamb will suffocate. That is why it's good to be around during the births if at all possible, to wipe away the mucus and birth sack with a handful of straw. The legs or necks of lambs can also become twisted in the birth canal. On those occasions, my father lay on the ground, half his forearm lost in a ewe, feeling his way in the mysterious, bloody dark.

More often than not, things were relatively fine. The lambs sprang up eagerly, bleating excitedly at every new chance to play. They popped into the air from a standstill, then raced around and around the hayrack in a joyous, woolly pack, their mothers looking on in exhausted, peevish annoyance.

We went through six crazed weeks of immunizations, castrations, and tail docking. The tails were easier, both on the lambs and us. Some farmers knotted on a rubber band and left it there until the tail fell off by itself. But my father bought a special tool for this purpose, shaped like a pair of pliers. He snipped a tail just below the anus, with more Blood Stopper sprinkled on to stem the flow of blood.

After about eight weeks, the lambs were weaned, sectioned off in a pen of their own with special high-nutrient pellets at mealtimes. The lambs and ewes cried for a day, calling for each other over the fences. But then they settled down, as if all memory vanished.

I only had one lamb die in my arms, an amazing sensation that even now I can remember: a steady, brave breath in a small, woolly frame, knock-kneed and with adorable velvet ears and a lovely muzzle. I held her (or was it a he? I no longer can remember this detail) in my lap, sitting on an old wooden straight-backed chair that long ago had lost its back, yellow paint chips coming off in a shower. The mother sat nearby under a big aluminum heat lamp with another lamb. My parents were in the house; it was just the sheep and I, breathing in the winter air, the collective sound of our exhalations calm and comforting. I stroked the tiny creature, the lanolin from its new wool coming off on my hands. She had not been well from the beginning, would not eat. She slept, her breathing sharp and ragged. Then the lamb let out a great sigh as though in exhaustion and—just like you always read about—died. I stood to carry her away, and the mother lifted her head to look at me, not making any sign of distress or opposition.

The lambs were sold by the end of March, usually in time for Easter dinners. My parents and I never said much as we rounded up the lambs and loaded them into the back of the pickup truck. The ewes screamed and the lambs called out. We drove to the auction house in a miserable silence, turning around from time to time to check on the lambs. They stood in a terrified pack at the back of the truck. When we got there, a man opened a gate to an empty pen and we lowered the tailgate. The lambs ran into the pen, thinking it was the way out. Then the man closed the gate and handed my father a receipt.

We kept Eric, the ram, in a stall around the corner from the ewes. In the interests of birth control, Eric was kept in solitary confinement until the appropriate breeding season. So most of the time he was very bored. Out of despair and idleness, he began charging and banging his head against the beams around his stall, always venting his energy on the same boards until he threatened to systematically destroy an entire corner of the barn and cause an avalanche. My father tried reinforcing the beams with other boards, but Eric broke those, too. He tossed his water bucket around, soaking his stall repeatedly and annoying my mother, who took the bucket away from him, only giving him water when she was there to stand and hold the bucket for him. Finally, my father came up with the idea to line the floor of Eric's stall with old rubber tires, breaking Eric's stride so he couldn't get up enough speed to do any appreciable damage.

Periodically, we trimmed his pale horns, which curved around his head artfully like a nautilus but threatened us with real injury when allowed to grow too long. So we rolled Eric over on his side, and I straddled his belly to weigh down his rump. I slipped an old towel around his head, covering his eyes, and he calmed immediately. Eric remained still the whole time my father filed away at the horns with a hacksaw.

This all seems very long ago. I went to college, got a newspaper job in Akron, and, eventually, fled to New York. My parents phased out the sheep and planted shallots to sell to high-end grocery stores. Then they gave that up as well and kept a small garden, amusing themselves by lining up dozens of enormous Chinese winter melons in the garage and in the bed of the pickup truck. The dog died of old age, and my father buried her near the septic tank, where my mother looked out the kitchen window to keep an eye on her.

My parents sold all the sheep except three: Twiggy, a friendly black-and-white-faced ewe who always became frighteningly thin after giving birth; Dai Ga Jeah (Cantonese for "older sister"), who was a sweet-natured thing; and Fuzzy, who surely had been one of our most adorable lambs, marked with a big gray spot on her side. Fuzzy, however, grew up to be bossy and bitchy and rammed the other two ladies aside every time my mother went in to feed them. After a while, Fuzzy became so irritable that my mother had to hold her at bay with a stick until the other two ewes had a chance to eat something. The three sheep lived on the farm for more than six additional years, growing enormous in their dirty, gray clouds of wool and eating acres of grass, which they could never hope to finish. My mother used the three remaining sheep as a kind of dispose-all, giving them apples that fell from a tree near the house and enormous, overripe squash from her garden.

But just after the dog died in the autumn of 1996, it rained solidly for two days. My mother, feeling ill, did not venture out. When the sky cleared, my mother went out to the barn and found it eerily quiet, clots of wool strewn throughout the pen. She peered through the open gate and caught sight of the three sheep, their rigid bodies just outside the door to the pasture. They had been tortured and mauled, their legs ripped and crusted with dried blood, their ears torn off, their muzzles gashed. They lay very closely to one another, within ten feet of the barn. My parents reported the incident to the sheriff's department, and the dog warden came after a day and a half, holding a clipboard. She inspected the bodies and looked at the prints in the dried mud.

No, it wasn't coyotes, she said. Just dogs.

Our own dog was never a sheep dog, but she must have done her duty for the fifteen years my parents had her. She had a very keen sense of hearing, and certainly would have alerted the house had she heard the intruders. Also, dogs are very respectful of territory, and outsiders never would have dared to venture into the barn.

So the warden gave my parents a form to fill out, and the county gave them fifty dollars a head for their loss. One by one, my parents loaded up the stiff corpses in the front bucket of the orange tractor and carried them to the end of the cornfield, where my father buried them in a long and deep trench. When he noticed, several days later, that something had made an attempt to dig up the bodies, my father scattered ashes from their garbage burn pit, and the graves were not touched again. It snowed and rained, washing away most signs of the carnage. On my next visit to the farm, my mother pointed out the places where the sheep had lain: There, she said; I followed her finger to a large gray stone. There. And there.

The destruction did not end there. A great oak tree with the diameter of a small car had stood for decades in the sheep paddock. Shortly after the sheep were killed, it relinquished its guardianship of the field and, weakened by years of termites tunneling in its core, collapsed into the corn with a dramatic gasp, flinging its branches in an enormous circumference. It was as though it tried to bury itself, throwing its weight into the earth with such force that it left a deep imprint in the cornfield. Bit by bit, my parents, who are in their sixties and seventies, hacked it up and stacked logs in front of the barn. There was enough firewood for years.

My parents became grayer and slower. They knew they had to give up the farm sooner or later, and for years only made desultory attempts at going through the boxes stored in the basement. Moving to the farm had been an act of rebellion against convention; leaving it would be an acquiescence to mortality.

But then my father had a heart attack and was flown by helicopter to a large hospital in Akron that could handle such cases. Doctors cracked open his chest, tore out a vein from the length of his right calf, and used this vessel to reroute the blood in his heart. My father had a long but steady recovery; he moved about the house slowly, clasping a small pillow to his chest so that if he sneezed, the sutures would not burst open. After my father was well, my parents sold the farm and bought a small house in Wooster, a five-minute walk from the hospital. Once again they are on a corner lot, bordered by a small evergreen on one side and a tiny spit of a creek on the other. My parents keep all their shades drawn but enjoy spying on their neighbors through the gaps between the window frames and the curtains; they use a pair of fancy binoculars that my father said he purchased for bird-watching after he retired. In her letters, my mother writes to me about the comings and goings of people around them. She no longer has ulcers. My father treats her with a tenderness that he never showed before, holding my mother's hand and making sure that she keeps out of the wind.

One beauty of country life is how uncomplicated the world becomes; but life factored out to its fundamentals just means there are fewer distractions on the way to death. I live in the city now, yet I remember vividly how I once lived so closely to the earth; it is an intimacy I crave. A farm breathes with memory, a collective presence of things once living—all those animals, all that rawness of the natural world. My experience with farming is modest, only two years' worth before I escaped into my education. Yet even a casual mention can send me to furtive weeping now. I am haunted by the mere breath of sheep, silly and dim in a cloud of wool and an aura of disbelief. I miss them. Because ultimately it is more than this episode of rural life that has passed. I worry about my parents with an anxiousness specific to only children: in a continent populated by three, the probability of solitude is vast. I think about the coming winter. I think about how cold it will be, how the air will be painful in the lungs. My eyes will hurt, and I fear I must step out alone into the metallic sharpness of night.

about the author

Her experiences growing up as an Asian American in Ohio's Amish country helped inform ANDREA LOUIE's novel, *Moon Cakes* (Ballantine Books, 1995). She is coeditor of *Topography of War: Asian American Essays* (Asian American Writers' Workshop, 2006) and communications manager for Religions for Peace, a UN-affiliated humanitarian organization based in New York. Louie has reviewed books for the *Chicago Tribune*, worked as a newspaper reporter in Ohio, and taught creative nonfiction in the youth programs at the Hamilton-Madison Settlement House in New York City's Chinatown and at the Asian American Writers' Workshop.

Louie is a member of the review panel in literature for the New York Council on the Arts and has served as a writer-in-residence for the National Book Foundation. In addition, she has been awarded a number of fellowships and artist residencies at Yaddo, the MacDowell Colony, Djerassi, Hedgebrook, and the Fundacíon Valparáiso in Spain. She lives in New York City.

Geese and Crows

Kathleen Dean Moore

BEREA

Kathleen with her father, Donald S. Dean

FRANK AND I MOVED WEST SO MANY

years ago, I'd forgotten how cold Ohio can be—wind charging up the riverbank, knocking the last leaves off the trees, tossing crows into wild flight. Here in the cemetery, crows skid sideways, then turn and sail downwind, flinching to avoid the fence. There's snow on this wind, rising rather than falling, wrapping white scarves around the graves. In a sudden gust, a garland of roses pinwheels by and lodges in a windrow of ribbons and plastic poinsettias. Beyond the fence, lines of geese roam the sky over the Sandusky River, forming and reforming like the folding edge of a flag.

Frank's great-great-grandfather came here more than a century ago, built a water mill close to where we're standing, bought farmland, planted celery in the black swamp soil. Moores have been here ever since, as solid a part of the town as the grindstone in the mill. Frank's father was a doctor here, tied to the town by life and death and generations of kindness. We all knew it would be hard for Frank's father to leave this place. Maybe that's why his mind had to go on ahead, leaving the body to follow reluctantly. He died at home with the TV on, a gradual death: flickering screen, falling snow, streetlights through the curtains, the snowplow thumping by.

Now his ashes will be buried in the soil and weighed down with a granite stone. It would not be right to scatter in the river a man so firmly rooted to this place, or cast him into the air to fly with the geese, each flake of him, like snow, hissing across the fields.

As we gathered for the interment, Frank told me that when his father was a boy, maybe fifteen, he decided to walk across the Sandusky River. This was not easily accomplished, because the river was deep behind the dam. Back then, there was no scuba gear. But very little stopped this man. Somehow he cut a hole in a galvanized tin bucket and welded in a window. Somehow he attached a hose connected to a bicycle pump. He rounded up some friends and a rowboat, tied rocks to his feet to keep himself from floating. Then he strapped the bucket over his head and walked into the river. As he shuffled along beneath twenty feet of silty water, his friends floated above him in the rowboat—one rowing, one pumping away to keep the bucket filled with air.

I could picture Frank's dad sitting on the rocky ledges to strap stones to his boots, a lanky kid with laughing friends gathered round. I can picture him clunking down the riverbank and down and down, until water rises over his head and the first bubbles break the clouded surface. What I can't imagine is how he must have felt to emerge dazed by light on the far side—bucket breaking the surface, shoulders suddenly heavy, sodden shirt-tail floating. Was he tempted to keep on walking, to shuffle up the bank and across the distances of fields flat to the edge of the earth? Did he wonder how light he would feel, hollow-boned as a heron, if he left behind his rock-bound boots, strode west into the wind, and never looked back? Nobody knows. The story says he just tightened the strings that held the rocks and walked back home underwater, trailing bubbles and silt.

His home is still here, on top of the hill. I struggled to get to sleep in that quiet house last night, and then the rumble of the snowplow woke me. The hall clock bonged each hour, as it has done since 1627, keeping time more reliably than the electric clock that blinks 12:00 every second, all night long.

The history that holds Frank's family to this place is heavy and layered: carpets on carpets, pillows on needlepoint pillows, slipcovers on silk upholstery on damask on horsehair, candles on burned-down stubs in brass candlesticks, and in the cupboard, new dishes stacked on sixty-year-old wedding dishes stacked on the great-grandparents' gold-rimmed china, the entire house filled with things, rafters to basement, and each thing filled with stories that now no one can tell.

On the granite stone in the cemetery, wind drives snow into the carved letters of Frank's father's name. Beyond the stone, a crow rides the wind. Even though the wind is strong enough to blow snow into the next county, the crow shrugs its shoulders, lifts its elbows, and floats. Only the strength of the wind keeps the crow in this place, suspended behind the preacher, who closes the Bible and bows his head. "Both now and forever more," he says. Geese string out low on the horizon, flying before the wind into the last streak of light between the clouds.

I don't know what tells the geese they need to go, the milling geese anxious to be somewhere else, circling the sky, weighing winter storms against the promise of something better. And what holds the crows, nesting each year in the pignut at the bottom of the ravine, pecking and flinching in the fallen leaves? Some people stay where they're born, some go somewhere else, and all of them, in the end, cross the river.

I DON'T REMEMBER SAYING good-bye to Frank's father when we moved to Oregon. I don't remember telling him we were leaving. Twenty-two years old, married, done with school: it was time to go. I don't know what he thought, to lose his son to a place so empty and far away. All I remember is staring from behind frantic windshield wipers into a night darker and wetter than any I had ever seen. When we crossed the Snake River into Oregon, our voices almost drowned in a night thunderous with rain. I imagined the empty space of us in his family's bright dining room in Ohio, his father at the big table, warm kitchen air and the smell of baked potatoes pouring into two empty chairs pulled back against the wall.

MY MOTHER CAME TO Ohio from England, carrying only a doll's cradle. My father came to Ohio from Michigan, with only a botany degree. They accumulated almost nothing, and most of what they had when they died, my sisters and I divided up and carried away on DC-7s routed to our homes in Oregon, Washington, Pennsylvania. The cradle. A hand lens. *A Field Guide to Ponds and Streams.* When the house was empty, we sold it and everything that was left, even the apple tree my father had grafted to bloom white on the west side, pink on the east, and the nest of doves in the lilac tree.

My father had been the naturalist at the Trailside Museum, in the beech-maple woods under the western approach to the Cleveland airport. With his pet crow on his shoulder, he led people beside Rocky River, hushing their chatter to listen to wrens, poking with sticks at strings of algae, sniffing at muskrat mud piles. He dredged knee-deep through warm water, through the smell of the river, fetid, algae-green, ticking with dragonfly wings, sticky with mosquitoes and jewelweed, and brought back a bucket of water. Everyone pressed around to see what they could see, mysteries dredged up from a place hidden to us.

I never understood why my parents, so in love with that river, arranged for their ashes to be interred in a brick wall in their church. In any event, the preacher pushed an envelope of their ashes through a mail slot between the bricks, first my mother, then ten years later, my father. It seemed wrong to me, I told the church receptionist at his funeral, that people who had lived so lightly and died with so few regrets, people as thin and joyous as birdsong, would now be bricked inside a chimney of ash.

The receptionist thought hard, her cheeks flushing. "There isn't much room in the wall, you know," she confided. "So only a pinch of each person goes into the envelope."

"Where is the rest of my parents?"

She looked hard at me, dropped her eyes. "Generally, we put extra ashes in the trash cans behind the church. I suppose they go to the landfill."

My mind flooded with the smell of cabbages rotting in the rain and the rush of gulls' wings, that flurry of white feathers, and the calls of gulls scattered like blown snow over the mounds of trash. I didn't know what to think of my mother and father flying so completely away. But they would like that, to be taken up into the body of a migratory bird, their calcium crusting against the open spaces in the bones that lift its wings. And if they stayed for a while in the landfill, I don't think they would mind that—just a dogleg in their journey into what my father called "the stream of living things."

When you die, my father told us, all the elements of your body will wash back into the stream. I pictured Tinkertoy calcium molecules and fortified nutrients tumbling end over end in a riffle, oxygen eddying around submerged rocks, nitrogen pouring over the lip of a rocky ford, all drifting downstream into some other life, an oak tree maybe, or a nestling crow. "You don't *cross* a river to a new place when you die," he told us. "You *become* the river."

DESPITE THE SKIFF OF snow, Frank and I easily find the trail leading down to Rocky River and the Trailside Museum. The days are short this late in November. Low sun casts lines across the path.

The winter I was ten, the river rose in flood between sandstone walls, lifting a carpet of sticks and dead leaves rimed with snow. It looked like solid ground to me. There was a red ball there: I remember that. So I stepped off the wall to get it and dropped into icy water that closed over my head. I don't remember being cold. I remember struggling to breathe.

I flailed through ice and fallen limbs and finally climbed a willow. That's where I was, clinging like a chickadee to a swaying branch, when my father rescued me.

Now here's the river, low and shining like tinfoil, and the familiar shush of dried leaves on the trail, the cold-toast smell. From the west runway, a plane rumbles toward an overcast sky already streaked with geese. A crow calls, then flaps into a hickory tree, rattling the branches. Only a few leaves dent the slick of the river, bending the reflection of bare gray trunks.

"Shh. Listen. A nuthatch."

It takes a moment for my heart to stop racing, but it's Frank who has said this, not my father. I choose a skipping stone from a shale bank, turn it in my hand, then lean down and skim it low and hard over the river. It skips once, twice, stumbles, and sinks. Water closes over the space where the stone has fallen through, the way the present closes over the past and leaves a river that flat, that still.

about the author

KATHLEEN DEAN MOORE is best known as the author of essays that explore our cultural and spiritual connections to wet, wild places: *Riverwalking: Reflections on Moving Water* (Lyons and Burford, 1995), *Holdfast: At Home in the Natural World* (Lyons Press, 1999), and *The Pine Island Paradox* (Milkweed Editions, 2004). *Riverwalking* won a Pacific Northwest Booksellers Association Book Award and was a finalist for an Oregon Book Award; *Holdfast* was granted the 2000 Sigurd Olson Nature Writing Award. *The Pine Island Paradox* is the 2005 winner of the Oregon Book Award.

Ohio's rivers taught Moore to love water, which she found so abundantly in Oregon when she and her husband, Frank, moved to that state. A Distinguished Professor of Philosophy at Oregon State University, she teaches environmental ethics and the philosophy of nature and directs the Spring Creek Project for Ideas, Nature, and the Written Word.

Answers

Mary Oliver

MAPLE HEIGHTS

Mary Oliver in Cleveland, 1979 (Molly Malone Cook photo)

The Black Walnut Tree

My mother and I debate:
we could sell
the black walnut tree
to the lumberman,
and pay off the mortgage.
Likely some storm anyway
will churn down its dark boughs,
smashing the house. We talk
slowly, two women trying
in a difficult time to be wise.
Roots in the cellar drains,
I say, and she replies
that the leaves are getting heavier
every year, and the fruit
harder to gather away.
But something brighter than money
moves in our blood—an edge
sharp and quick as a trowel
that wants us to dig and sow.
So we talk, but we don't do
anything. That night I dream
of my fathers out of Bohemia
filling the blue fields
of fresh and generous Ohio
with leaves and vines and orchards.
What my mother and I both know
is that we'd crawl with shame
in the emptiness we'd made
in our own and our fathers' back yard.
So the black walnut tree
swings through another year

of sun and leaping winds,
of leaves and bounding fruit,
and, month and month, the whip-
crack of the mortgage.

Spring in the Classroom

Elbows on dry books, we dreamed
Past Miss Willow Bangs, and lessons, and windows,
To catch all day glimpses and guesses of the greening
    woodlot,
Its secrets and increases,
Its hidden nests and kind.
And what warmed in us was no book-learning,
But the old mud blood murmuring,
Loosening like petals from bone sleep.
So spring surrounded the classroom, and we suffered to be
    kept indoors,
Droned through lessons, carved when we could with
    jackknives
Our pulsing initials into the desks, and grew
Angry to be held so, without pity and beyond reason,
By Miss Willow Bangs, her eyes two stones behind glass,
Her legs thick, her heart
In love with pencils and arithmetic.

So it went—one gorgeous day lost after another
While we sat like captives and breathed the chalky air
And the leaves thickened and birds called
From the edge of the world—till it grew easy to hate,
To plot mutiny, even murder. Oh, we had her in chains,
We had her hanged and cold, in our longing to be gone!
And then one day, Miss Willow Bangs, we saw you
As we ran wild in our three o'clock escape
Past the abandoned swings; you were leaning
All furry and blooming against the old brick wall
In the Art Teacher's arms.

Answers

If I envy anyone it must be
My grandmother in a long ago
Green summer, who hurried
Between kitchen and orchard on small
Uneducated feet, and took easily
All shining fruits into her eager hands.

That summer I hurried too, wakened
To books and music and circling philosophies.
I sat in the kitchen sorting through volumes of answers
That could not solve the mystery of the trees.

My grandmother stood among her kettles and ladles.
Smiling, in faulty grammar,
She praised my fortune and urged my lofty career.
So to please her I studied—but I will remember always
How she poured confusion out, how she cooled and labeled
All the wild sauces of the brimming year.

about the author

MARY OLIVER has been writing poetry for nearly five decades, and in that time she has become America's foremost voice on our experience of the physical, natural world. As poet Archibald MacLeish once wrote to her, "You have indeed entered the kingdom. You have done something better than create your own world: you have discovered the world we all live in and do not see and cannot feel."

Born in Maple Heights, Oliver was raised in a world of woods, farms, and horses, a natural world that has stayed with her ever since. She has published more than twenty volumes of poetry and prose, including *American Primitive* (Little, Brown, 1983), a poetry collection which won the 1984 Pulitzer Prize, and *New and Selected Poems* (Beacon Press, 1992; a second volume appeared in 2005), which won the National Book Award.

Oliver lives in Provincetown, on Cape Cod, alone since the 2005 death of her partner, Molly Malone Cook.

After the Flood

Scott Russell Sanders

PORTAGE COUNTY

Scott Sanders and his collie, Rusty

A RIVER POURED THROUGH THE

landscape I knew as a child. It was the power of the place, gathering rain and snowmelt, surging through the valley under sun, under ice, under the bellies of fish and the curled brown boats of sycamore leaves. You will need a good map of Ohio to find the river I am talking about, the west branch of the Mahoning. The stretch of it I knew best no longer shows on maps, a stretch that ran between wooded slopes and along the flanks of cornfields and pastures in the township of Charlestown, in Portage County, a rural enclave surrounded by the smokestacks and concrete of Akron, Youngstown, and Cleveland in the northeastern corner of the state.

Along that river bottom I gathered blackberries and hickory nuts, trapped muskrats, rode horses, followed baying hounds on the scent of raccoons. Spring and fall, I walked barefoot over the tilled fields, alert for arrowheads. Along those slopes I helped a family of Swedish farmers collect buckets of maple sap. On the river itself I skated in winter and paddled in summer, I pawed through gravel bars in search of fossils, I watched hawks preen and pounce, I courted and canoed and idled. This remains for me a primal landscape, imprinted on my senses, a place by which I measure every other place.

It is also, now, a drowned landscape. In the early 1960s, when I was in high school, politicians and bankers and realtors ordained that the Mahoning should be snared. A dam was built, the river died, and water backed up over most of the land I knew. No city needed the water for drinking. The reservoir, named after a man who had never lived in that valley, provided owners of loud boats with another playground for racing and waterskiing, and provided me with a lesson in loss. If the loss were mine alone, the story would not be worth telling. My grieving for a drowned landscape is private, a small ache in a bruised world. But the building of the dam, the obliteration of that valley, the displacement of people and beasts, these were public acts, the sort of acts we have been repeating from coast to coast as we devour the continent.

Like many townships in farm country, remote from the offices where the fate of land is decided, Charlestown has suffered more than one erasure. Long before the building of the reservoir, the government had already sliced away the northern third of the township for an arsenal, a wild, murderous place I have written about in *The Paradise of Bombs*. On current maps of the township that upper third is blank white, and most of the remaining two-thirds, flooded by the reservoir, is vacant blue. Merely by looking at the map, one can tell that here is a sacrificial zone.

~

Returning to one's native ground, always tricky, becomes downright treacherous when the ground is at the bottom of a lake. Unwilling to dive through so much water, I can return to that drowned landscape, as I can return to childhood, only by diving through memory.

I had just become a teenager when the government began purchasing the farms and trailers and shacks that would be in the path of the reservoir. (If there had been mansions and factories in the way, the politicians would have doomed a different valley.) Among the first to be unhoused was the Swedish family, old Mr. Sivy and his two unmarried children, who had farmed that bottom land with big-shouldered horses, whose silage I had pitchforked in the steaming silo, whose cows I had fed, whose maple syrup I had savored hot from the vat. Uprooted, the old man soon died. The children bought a new farm on high ground, trying to start over, but it was no good, the soil too thin, worn out, no black bottom land, no fat maples, no river pouring through it. All down the valley it was the same, people forced to move by a blizzard of government paper, occasionally by the sheriff, in a few instances by the arrival of bulldozers at their front door.

While gangs of men with dynamite and dump trucks tore down the condemned buildings, other gangs with earthmovers and cement mixers slowly raised a wall across the river. For a year I watched it rise, while I wooed a girl who lived on a ridge overlooking the dam site. Crooners purred love songs from the stereo in her parlor, against an accompaniment of chuffs and shouts and whistles from the valley below. I studied the contours of that girl's face while the river's contours were bullied into the shape of blueprints. The huge concrete forms, the Tinkertoy scaffolds, the blasting, the snort of compressors, the lurch of heavy machines are confused in me now with the memory of damp hands and lingering kisses. The girl and I broke up, but the concrete held. Thereafter, I avoided that ridge, and did not see the laying of the dam's final tier, did not see the steel gates close. By the time I graduated from high school, water was beginning to lap over the banks of the Mahoning, but I could not bear to go down to the river and look.

When I left Ohio for college, my family left as well, trailing my father's work to Louisiana. My childhood friends dispersed—to war, to jail, to distant marriages and jobs, to cities where lights glittered and dollars sang. I had scant reason to visit that flooded township and good reason to keep my distance. Why rush to see a muddy expanse of annihilating water?

~

Some years later, however, duties carried me through the northeastern corner of Ohio, within an hour's drive of my old neighborhood. I had not planned to make a detour. Yet the names of towns emblazoned on huge green signs along the highway tugged at me. The shapes of chimneys and roofs, the colors of barns, the accents in fast-food booths and gas stations, all drew me off the interstate onto the roads of Portage County, up the stream of recollection toward that childhood place.

The season of my return was late winter, after the last snow and before the first plowing, before grass resumed its green sizzle, before trees blurred with leaves. The shape of the land lay exposed. It was a gray day, a day to immunize one against nostalgia, a day safe, I supposed, for facing up to what I had lost. Surely I was prepared by now to see the great erasure. I was a man and had put behind me a boy's affection for a stretch of river and a patch of dirt. New places had claimed me, thereby loosening the grip of that old landscape. Still, to ease my way back, before going to the reservoir I drove through the county seat, Ravenna, which had scarcely changed, and then through Edinburgh, Atwater, Deerfield, Palmyra, Paris, Wayland—tiny crossroad settlements where I had played baseball and eaten pie and danced—and these, too, had scarcely changed. Circling, I drew closer and closer to the blue splotch on the map.

The best way to approach the water, I decided, was along the road where, for half our years in Charlestown, my family had lived on five acres with horses and rabbits and dogs. Surely our gray-shingled house would still be there, safe on its ridge above the lake, even if most of the land I had known was drowned. So I turned from the highway onto that curving, cracked, tar-slick road, looking for the familiar. But at the corner, where there should have been a farmhouse, a silo, a barn, there was only a billboard marking the entrance to the West Branch Reservation. The fields where I had baled hay now bristled with a young woods. There was no house in the hollow where the road dipped down, where the family of Seventh Day Adventists used to live with their stacks of apocalyptic pamphlets and their sad-eyed children. The spinster's white bungalow was gone, along with the battered bus in the side yard, which had served her for a chicken coop. Yard after yard had grown up in brush, and the shade trees spread darkness over their own seedlings. No mailboxes leaned on posts beside the road, no driveways broke the fringe of weeds. The trailer park was gone, the haunted house was gone, the tar-paper shanty where the drunk mechanic beat his wife and the wife beat her kids and the kids wailed, that was gone, and so was every last trailer and cottage and privy and shack, all down the blacktopped mile to our place.

I recognized our place by the two weeping willows out front. My father and I had planted those willows from slips, had fenced them round to protect the tender bark from deer, had watered and weeded and nursed them along. By the day of my visit those twigs had burgeoned into yellow fountains some fifty feet high, brimming over the woods that used to be our cleared land, woods that flourished where our house and barn had stood. I did not get out of the car. I could see from the road all that I was ready to see. The dense thicket, bare of leaves, was the color of rusty iron. Aside from the willows, no hint of our work or ownership survived.

I felt a fool. During the years of my absence, while my mind had suffered the waters to rise through the forest and up the ravines onto the margins of our land, I had preserved the gray-shingled house, the low white barn, the lilacs and forsythia, the orchard and pasture, the garden, the lawn. And yet, all the while, cedar and sumac and brambles, like the earth's dark fur, had been pushing up through my past.

Sight of the reservoir, surely, could not be worse. I continued down the road through the vigorous woods. Not a house, not a barn, not a plowed field. The first clearing I came to was half a mile farther on, at the spot where a man named Ferry had lived. He used to let the neigh-borhood kids swim in his pond, even after a boastful boy dived into a rock and drowned. We knew that when we knocked at Mr. Ferry's door, raising money for school or scouts, he would buy whatever we had to sell. He was a tender man. He loved his wife so much that when she died, he planted a thousand white pines in her memory. The pines, spindly in my recollection, had grown into a forest by the day of my return.

In place of Mr. Ferry's house and yard there was a state campground now, encircled by the spiky green palisade of pines. The entrance booth was boarded up. A placard outside instructed campers to deposit their fees—so much for trailers, so much for tents—in the box below. There was no box below, only a slab of plywood with ragged holes from which the screws had been ripped. Nor were there any campers on this wintry afternoon. As I drove through the vacant lot, the only sounds were the crunch of gravel beneath my tires and the yawp of blue jays overhead and the shoosh of wind through the pines.

I pulled away from the campground and drove on. My mind raced ahead along the road as I remembered it, steeply downhill between fat maples and patchy sycamores to the river and the steel-girdered bridge. I had rolled down that hill in a school bus, swayed down on horseback, hurtled down on bicycle and sled, run down on foot. The slope and feel of it, fixed inside me, became my standard for all hills. From the bridge I had watched the river's current raveling over sandbars, minnows flick-ering in the shallows, water-striders dimpling the surface. Now and again, when the sun was right, I had spied my own face peering up from the stream. In memory, the road stretched on beyond the bridge, passing the tin-roofed shed where the maple syrup boiled, passing the Sivy farm, rising up the far slope to a T-junction with a ridgeline road. Turn left from there, and I would go to the high school. Turn right, and I would go to the barbershop and feed store. As my thoughts raced ahead of the car, inside me the valley opened and the river flexed its long sleek muscle.

Rounding the curve, however, I had to slam on the brakes to avoid running into a guardrail that blocked the road. Beyond the railing, where valley and bridge and river should have been, flat gray water spread away toward distant hills. You know this moment from dreams: You are in a familiar room, but when you turn to leave, where a door should be there is a wall; or you come up behind someone you love, speak her name, yet when she turns around her face is blank; or you find the story of the universe written on a page, but when you draw close to read it, the letters dissolve. Waters of separation, waters of oblivion, waters of death.

I got out of the car and pressed my thighs against the cold steel barricade and stared. Gray, flat, empty lake. Not even a boat to redeem the emptiness. A lone crow slowly pumped toward the horizon on glossy black wings. Along the shore, a few sycamores still thrust up their mottled branches. Except for those trees, the pavement beneath my boots, and hills too high for water to claim, everything I knew had been swept away.

My worst imaginings had failed to prepare me for this. I stood there dazed. I could not take it in, so much had been taken away. For a long spell I leaned against the guardrail and dredged up everything I could remember of what lay beneath the reservoir. But memory was at last defeated by the blank gray water. No effort of mind could restore the river or drain the valley. I surrendered to what my eyes were telling me. Only then was I truly exiled.

~

Those who built the dam had their reasons. You have heard the litany: flood control, recreation, development. I very much doubt that more human good has come from that muddy, silting, rarely frequented lake than came from the cultivated valley and wild woods and free-flowing river. I am suspicious of the logic that would forestall occasional floods by creating a permanent one. But I do not wish to debate the merits of dams. I mean only to speak of how casually, how relentlessly we sever the bonds between person and place.

One's native ground is the place where, since before you had words for such knowledge, you have known the smells, the seasons, the birds and beasts, the human voices, the houses, the ways of working, the lay of the land, and the quality of light. It is the landscape you learn before you retreat inside the illusion of your skin. You may love the place if you flourished there, or hate the place if you suffered there. But love it or hate it, you cannot shake free. Even if you move to the antipodes, even if you become intimate with new landscapes, you still bear the impression of that first ground.

I am all the more committed to know and care for the place I have come to as an adult because I have lost irretrievably the childhood landscapes that gave shape to my love of the earth. The farm outside Memphis where I was born has vanished beneath parking lots and the poison-perfect lawns of suburbs. The arsenal, with its herds of deer grazing on the grassy roofs of ammunition bunkers, is locked away behind chain-link fences, barbed wire, and guns. And the Mahoning Valley has been drowned. In our century, in our country, no fate could be more ordinary.

Of course, in mourning the drowned valley I also mourn my drowned childhood. The dry land preserved the traces of my comings and goings; the river carried the reflection of my beardless face. Yet even as a boy I knew that landscape was incomparably older than I, and richer, and finer. Some of the trees along the Mahoning had been rooted there when the first white settlers arrived from New England. Hawks had been hunting and deer had been drinking there since before our kind harnessed oxen. The gravels, laden with fossils, had been shoved there ten thousand years ago by glaciers. The river itself was the offspring of glaciers, a channel for meltwater to follow toward the Ohio, and thence to the Mississippi and the Gulf of Mexico. What I knew of the land's own history made me see that expanse of water as a wound.

Loyalty to place arises from sources deeper than narcissism. It arises from our need to be at home on the earth. We marry ourselves to the creation by knowing and cherishing a particular place, just as we join ourselves to the human family by marrying a particular man or woman. If the marriage is deep, divorce is painful. My drive down that unpeopled road and my desolate watch beside the reservoir gave me a hint of what others must feel when they are wrenched from their place. I say a *hint* because my loss is mild compared to what others have lost.

I think of the farmers who saw their wood lots and fields go under the flood. I think of the Miami and Shawnee who spoke of belonging to that land as a child belongs to a mother, and who were driven out by white soldiers. I think of the hundred other tribes that were herded onto reservations far from the graves of their ancestors. I think of the Africans who were yanked from their homes and bound in chains and shipped to this New World. I think about refugees, set in motion by hunger or tyranny or war. I think about children pushed onto the streets by cruelty or indifference. I think about migrant workers, dust bowl émigrés, all the homeless wanderers. I think about the poor everywhere— and it is overwhelmingly the poor—whose land is gobbled by strip mines, whose neighborhoods are wiped out by highways and shopping malls, whose villages are destroyed by bombs, whose forests are despoiled by chain saws and executive fountain pens.

The word "nostalgia" was coined in 1688 as a medical term, to provide an equivalent for the German word meaning homesickness. We commonly treat homesickness as an ailment of childhood, like mumps or chickenpox, and we treat nostalgia as an affliction of age. On our lips, nostalgia usually means a sentimental regard for the trinkets and fashions of an earlier time, for an idealized past, for a vanished youth. We speak of a nostalgia for the movies of the 1930s, say, or the haircuts of the 1950s. It is a shallow use of the word. The two Greek roots of "nostalgia" literally mean "return pain." The pain comes not from returning home but from longing to return. Perhaps it is inevitable that a nation of immigrants—who shoved aside the native tribes of this continent, who enslaved and transported Africans, who still celebrate motion as if humans were dust motes—that such a nation should lose the deeper meaning of this word. A footloose people, we find it difficult to honor the lifelong, bone-deep attachment to place. We are slow to acknowledge the pain in yearning for one's native ground, the deep anguish in not being able, ever, to return.

On a warmer day I might have taken off my clothes and stepped over the guardrail and waded on down that road under the lake. Where the water was too deep, I could have continued in a boat, letting down a line to plumb the bottom. I would not be angling for death, which is far too easy to catch, but for life. To touch the ground even through a length of rope would be some consolation. The day was cold, however, and I was far from anyone who knew my face. So I climbed into the car and turned away and drove back through the resurgent woods.

about the author

Versatile and prolific, SCOTT RUSSELL SANDERS has won much acclaim for his novels, collections of short stories, creative nonfiction, personal essays, and children's books. His most recent books are *Hunting for Hope* (Beacon Press, 1998), *The Country of Language* (Milkweed Editions, 1999), *The Force of Spirit* (Beacon Press, 2000), and *A Private History of Awe* (Farrar, Straus and Giroux, 2006), a memoir.

His work has been selected for *The Best American Essays*, the *Kenyon Review* Award for Literary Excellence, the PEN Syndicated Fiction Award, and the John Burroughs Essay Award; it has been honored by the American Library Association and the National Council of Teachers of English; it has been twice nominated for the National Magazine Award; and it has won the Lannan Literary Award. His fiction and essays have been reprinted in *The Norton Reader*, *The Art of the Personal Essay*, *The Dolphin Reader*, *The Riverside Reader*, *The Harper and Row Reader*, and more than fifty other anthologies. He has been awarded fellowships from the Guggenheim Foundation, the National Endowment for the Arts, and the Lilly Endowment. He is a contributing editor to *Audubon* magazine.

A professor of English at Indiana University since 1971, he has received the Frederick Bachman Lieber Award for Distinguished Teaching, the highest such award given at the university. He is married with two grown children, Eva and Jesse.

Salamanders and Sycamores

A Natural History

Jeffery Smith

MONROE COUNTY

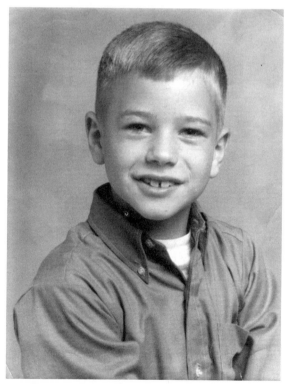

Jeffery Smith

I WAS BORN LUCKY, THIRTY-SEVEN YEARS ago, in the Ohio River valley town of New Martinsville, West Virginia. Just across the river in the Appalachian foothills of southeastern Ohio, both my mother's family and my father's family had settled generations before, and—this was my great good fortune—all those years later we were still planted there. My mother had been born and raised up in Stillhouse Hollow—"Holler," in the local parlance—outside the village of Clarington, and among my first memories is a June evening in that hollow. It would have been 1965, since my mother was pregnant with my brother Jim. I was in the root cellar with my Grandma Thomas, helping her shelve the jam she'd canned earlier that afternoon, when Grandpa called down the stairs: "Let's get you outside and run the stink off your bones before it gets dark."

Even in the summer, in that hollow ringed by hills, we lost the sun early, so we ran out into the yard and went straight for the pasture field. The coonhounds followed us, down the pathway that led from the porch stoop out past the garden and the barn, and then beyond to the cornfield, the potato patch, and the chicken coop. Finally we were in the pasture. There we angled right, toward Stillhouse Run, and I ambled along its bank from one sycamore to another, careening in broad semi-circles out away from them into the broad green expanse of the pasture, the coonhounds baying and barking as they ran. We circled the pasture, then retraced our path back to the house. Spent, I lay down in the cool, dew-washed grass before the porch. The dogs circled me. Their tongues on my face tickled me into peals of laughter. I sat up to attend to them one by one, as Grandpa had taught me, calling them to me by name. They were lanky and long-eared, firm-bodied and clear-eyed. Their hindquarters swayed with their wagging tails, and I stroked their ears, soft as velvet with the veins tracing down like rivulets of rain.

My grandfather could incite them to howl—their treeing voice, he called it—but try as I might, I couldn't hit the right note to bring this on. I rose to my feet, high-stepped through the rhubarb patch, and leaned against the damp stone foundation of the brooder house. My grandfather stood in a circle of gleaming beagles, blueticks, and black and tans, his profile and theirs silhouetted against the orange and lavender skies of twilight as those plaintive harmonies echoed and shivered up the hollow. Fireflies twinkled as if they would foreshadow the stars.

Now we moved to the porch. I sat there between my mom and her father on a small rocking chair, listening to the mourning doves out in the woods. I loved their haunted low drone. I breathed in deep. I loved the rich damp smell of this place: the air mixing together the pure amphibian smell of the Run with the smell of all the plants along its banks and in the forest that grew up the hillsides. Grandma, done finally with her work, sat beside Grandpa reading. I stood and climbed onto Grandpa's lap, lifted his hat off his head, and put it on my own. The Thomases were mostly Welsh—"Black Irish," as they were locally known—and what little hair Grandpa had left was the same coal-black, almost blue color as my mother's. They also shared the same olive-tinted skin and vivid, nearly opaque brown eyes.

On that June evening Mom was twenty-one, and I was three; I was a "shotgun baby," born six months after she and my father graduated from high school. We lived a few miles down the Ohio, in the village of Hannibal, along the state highway in a house trailer that was perched on cinder blocks; in high winds the roof had a tendency to come loose. Mom was raised in this house, and we came up here a couple of times during the week, and always on Sunday.

As a child I traipsed without tiring in the woods up Stillhouse Hollow—named after the moonshining operation that Jed Frankhauser used to run two miles upstream from my grandparents' place—with that grandfather, who seemed to know every tree in those woods, every animal track, and more stories than the Bible. I liked it here: up that hollow there wasn't any traffic to speak of, and things were quiet. I would pass hours wading in the Run, turning over rocks and trying to catch in my hands the salamanders and crawdads I'd find beneath them.

"Oh, am I hot," I heard my mother say, and I knew what that meant: she was going to walk down to the Run and stand in the water. She pushed herself up off her chair and held out her arm. I clasped her hand and we moved off the porch. As she stood in the water I lay out on that creek's bank, a dreaming and distracted child; and as I lay there the creek became a river, the river itself became sea, and the boy sprawled face-first there on the bank became salamander, became mourning dove, became sycamore.

Then I came back to myself, another creature of this place. I rolled to my feet, walked a couple feet up the bank, and leaned back against that sycamore. My mother stood in the cool water. I looked up to the hills that sheltered the hollow as they shone in the dusk. I looked down the Run to where it met up with the broad, slow-moving Ohio. I lifted my head and breathed in long and deep, trying to plant the smell of that place into my lungs.

Surely I couldn't imagine then that I'd ever want to live out of reach of those hills, in some place where I couldn't hear the Ohio sing down out of the hills and wash the valleys clean even while we slept. And I did leave that place, but in the small of my back I can feel that sycamore. That smell is in my lungs still. I hope as I lay dying its vapor will rise off my cooling blood and those hills, those trees, those creatures fill the room.

～

Four months after we moved to a suburban-style house in Schupbach Addition, thanks to my father's promotion to foreman at a chemical plant, I started school. Roughly half the kids in my class were "town kids" and the other half "hill kids," from back in the hills and hollows away from the more modern riverfront. Some of their fathers labored now in the plants, having swapped the farms and mines for a more steady income. Most, though, lived the way white people there have for generations: mining or farming. The hill kids every morning endured hour-long bus rides to school, and many wore hand-me-downs, and some of them brought into the classroom the rich scent of the barnyard.

From the start I preferred the company of the hill kids and went to their farms when I could, to spend weekends and overnights. In those farmhouses I would awaken at the crack of dawn, go out with my class-mates to gather the eggs and help with the milking, then come back inside to eat breakfast, the old smell of the houses all about us. As the sun began showing over the eastern hills, we would eat the freshly gathered eggs with bacon or ham from the hogs everybody raised, the radio inevitably tuned to WWVA out of Wheeling, which broadcast its blend of bluegrass, old-time country, and newer traditional country all over the central Appalachians and up into the Northeast as far as New England and eastern Canada. WWVA's early morning broadcasts were aimed at their large farming audience: in those hours they favored the old-time string band music and bluegrass, the farm families I stayed with would set into foot-tapping and occasionally whistling along with those tunes, then fall utterly silent when the farm market reports came over the airwaves. My own relatively citified feet could not resist that music, and I would wait out the market reports quietly impatient for it to resume. Sometimes on Saturday nights I would join my hill kid classmates at their barn dances. Everybody whose church didn't forbid dancing showed up—we passed our partners around and around, little boys like me and my classmates easily sharing a dance with our parents and grandparents while the local old-time string band played square dances and cakewalks.

Such remnants of our past were mostly getting away from us, though. As my Great-grandpa Thomas had foreseen, within a half generation life in Monroe County was thoroughly transformed. In those same years the Appalachian Regional Commission began to take an interest in us. Founded in 1964, this Great Society agency was charged with the task of raising our "deprived" lives to the American standard. It seems their idea of bettering life in the region was to train us to live elsewhere; the biggest part of the agency's budget went toward building roads that spidered us out of our hills toward Columbus and Charlotte and Detroit and Baltimore.

Having left the farm and rejected the mine, believing—accurately, as it turned out—that there was no future in either, my dad had no meaningful work to teach me. How do you mentor a son for factory work? Our world was changing, and it was left to my mother to show me how to fend in it. What she taught me to love is what I most love still. So this is what I did as a child, while the world outside changed its shape and tenor: I read; I plunged into creeks and overturned rocks on the banks, looking for lizards and crawdads; I walked in the woods, and I studied on the creatures of the ground. I leaned against trees. And I read some more.

about the author

JEFFERY SMITH's first book, *Where the Roots Reach for Water: A Personal and Natural History of Melancholia* (North Point Press, 1999), won the PEN/Albrand Art of the Memoir award. His book *Spinning Plastic Self: How Rock and Roll Shaped This Man* is forthcoming. Smith lives in Bozeman, Montana.

Toward a Literature of the Midwest

Mark Winegardner

A few years ago, sitting on a panel at the Midwestern Modern Language Association Conference in Cleveland, I asserted that there have been more great American writers from the Midwest than from the rest of the country put together.

At a literary gathering in New York, you can call New York the literary capital of America and people will stroke their chins and nod, irked only that you felt the need to say something so self-evident. Brag up Southern writers here in the South—at a literary gathering, a barbecue joint, a gas station, anywhere, and you can expect bourbon glasses raised in assent and at least one hoot of *"hell,* yeah!" But I started riffing on the preeminence of the midwestern writer *in* the Midwest, in front of people who taught English at a university somewhere in the Midwest (everyone but me, and I used to)—and the audience actually gasped. What about the South, you moron? What about New England? Ever hear of *New York?*

Nice places, I said. But from Missourian Mark Twain on (as Chicagoan Ernest Hemingway said, "All modern American literature comes from one book by Mark Twain called *Huckleberry Finn"*), the Midwest has been the largest supplier of high-test American lit.

As semi-accidental hyperbolic claims go (I was going to say that a *preponderance* of great American writers came from the Midwest; right before I did, I decided that "preponderance" was a really pretentious word, and thereby may have overstated things), this one's at least defensible.

Consider America's nine winners of the Nobel Prize in Literature. The first, Sinclair Lewis, was born and raised in Minnesota and set his best work in the Midwest. He's followed by Eugene O'Neill (token New Yorker), Pearl S. Buck (born in West Virginia, on the eastern cusp of the Midwest), T. S. Eliot (from St. Louis), William Faulkner (token Southerner), Ernest Hemingway (born in Chicago, forged by Michigan), John Steinbeck (token Californian), Saul Bellow (*The Adventures of Augie March* begins "I'm an American, Chicago-born"), and Toni Morrison (born and raised in Lorain).

That's 56 percent (I'm not counting Buck, who's not a Midwesterner and also not really a great writer)—more than the rest of America combined.

The Nobel is only one measure, of course. But add to those five writers the likes of F. Scott Fitzgerald (Minnesota), John Dos Passos (Chicago), Carl Sandburg (Illinois), Theodore Dreiser (Indiana), Thornton Wilder (Wisconsin), Marianne Moore (St. Louis), Tennessee Williams (raised in St. Louis), and Clevelanders Hart Crane and Langston Hughes. Add more recent writers (all of whom have won either the Pulitzer Prize or the National Book Award) like Minnesotan Tim O'Brien, Michiganders Theodore Roethke and Philip Levine, Iowan Mona Van Duyn, Illini Charles Johnson and Robert Olen Butler, Missourians James Tate, Jane Smiley, Carl Dennis, and Jonathan Franzen, and the Ohioans collected in this book.

This is (a) just scratching the surface and (b) defining the "Midwest" only as the five Great Lakes states (Ohio, Indiana, Michigan, Illinois, Wisconsin) and the three just across the Mississippi River (Minnesota, Iowa, Missouri) and not the plains states (which would weaken my argument anyway, since they don't contribute many greats once you get past Willa Cather and Ralph Ellison).

Despite being from the white-hot center of American literature, those of us who come from the Midwest or set our work there (or, worse, both) have to fight being pigeonholed as regional writers. Someone who sets twenty books in a four-block section of Manhattan would never be called "regional." But set twenty books in any twenty states that don't share a border with New York, and "regional writer" will sully the first sentence of your obituary.

This is, of course, because American publishing happens almost exclusively in New York, the most parochial big city in America.

A month after I finished my last novel, *Crooked River Burning*, I came to New York, at my publisher's request, to discuss how they were going to market, promote, and possibly even sell the book. Everyone's excited, I was told. Everyone *loves* it!

Whatever. It was my sixth book. Publishing six books teaches you to disregard praise of any sort. Still, I thought the book had turned out well. It's a love story, immersed in Cleveland history. What's not to like?

We went into a big conference room. The marketing director started the meeting by saying (after she admitted she hadn't read the novel), "We see this as a strong regional book." If it does well in the Midwest, she says, there's hope it may catch on elsewhere.

They all seemed surprised when I asked if the elevator went to the roof, so I could go jump off.

I hit the roof instead. A book like *Crooked River Burning* set in New York (say, Mark Helprin's *Winter's Tale* or Don DeLillo's *Underworld*) would never be called a "regional book." Yes, most Americans don't really care about Cleveland and how it got that way, but by and large, most Americans don't care about New York per se either, and we have to listen to that all the time.

I might as well have been speaking in tongues.

They did relent, a little, expanding my book tour to include the South as well (on the logic that I live there and it would be cheap).

Going on a book tour through the South taught me a lot. The South, suffused with the defiant fatalism of a conquered nation, is the only place where you can be branded a regional writer and not necessarily suffer for it. There are two good reasons for this, from which the Midwest could learn but never will.

First, the South supports its own. Bookstores shelve fiction in two principal places: "Fiction" and "Southern Writers." Often, "Southern Writers" occupies half the store: full of comfortable chairs, warm lighting, autographed pictures of any Southerner who ever typed the word "Mama." (My books are shelved in the dark, narrow aisles of "Fiction," where the only sound is the distant laughter of the cool kids over yonder in "Southern"; sometimes actual tumbleweeds blow by.) Likewise, at universities not only in the South but throughout America, there are, as you read this, thousands of students reading books for their Southern Literature classes, and hundreds of grad students pounding out dissertations in hopes of someday securing a job as some university's Southern-Lit person. Not to mention the various Institutes of Southern Culture. Not to mention the robust sales enjoyed by each annual edition of *New Stories from the South.*

Imagine a *New Stories from the Midwest.* Imagine an Institute of Midwestern Culture. Imagine if every university in the Midwest, and maybe elsewhere, offered a course in the Literature of the Midwest.

No one would buy it, no one would take it seriously, no one would take the class.

And that's just in the Midwest. That's *especially* in the Midwest.

If our bookstores started a "Midwestern Writers" section, they wouldn't put Hemingway, Bellow, or Morrison there. They wouldn't lug *The Things They Carried* there or reshelve *The Corrections.* Instead, there'd be coffee table books about nearby sports teams, books by local TV personalities, and vanity-press books placed there to get their persistent authors off the store managers' backs. If your book wound up in "Midwestern," even your mom wouldn't go there to buy it.

Which leads me to the second thing: Southerners may leave the South, but it never leaves them. Southern writers tend to set most of their work in the South. It's a part of southern culture to fight one's southernness as a youth and, eventually, succumb to it; this is a huge theme in southern writing and in the biographies of southern writers. Plus, sooner or later, nearly all southern writers settle in the South. Faulkner was chronologically but not actually a member of the Lost Generation. His longest stretch away from the South came in Hollywood, where he felt he had to go to generate cash to pay his bills back in Mississippi. Once that dalliance was over, he spent the rest of his life in the South. Flannery O'Connor went to Iowa for grad school, but, otherwise, rarely left Georgia. Eudora Welty spent almost a century living in the same Mississippi house where she was born.

In contrast, many of the Midwest's best writers grew up, went to Harvard or someplace equally designed to eradicate midwesternness, and spent the rest of their lives in New York or some place equally foreign, never to return. Some took this to extremes. Eliot's renouncement of his midwesternness was the most severe: he left St. Louis for Harvard, left Harvard for London, and a few years later became a British citizen. Hemingway set a book in Chicago and wrote nearly all his best work while in foreign countries. Hoosier Lew Wallace is the rare midwestern writer who saw the world and returned home, where he wrote novels like *Ben-Hur*, set in the waning years of the Roman Empire.

The Midwest *should* support its own.

Midwesterners *should* more often stay, either literally or metaphorically.

The Midwest *should* embrace its heritage.

None of these things will ever happen, and even if they do, they'll be done badly. The Midwest has no talent for such things. What comes off in the South as swagger, as defiance, as preservation of a distinct voice and history would, in the sausage-fingered hands of us midwesterners, come off as boosterism. Or (to use a word thrust into the language by the Midwest's first Nobel laureate) as Babbittry.

What the Midwest wants its sons and daughters to do is leave, accomplish big things in New York or L.A., and, ideally, say nice things about where they came from. (If Drew Carey hadn't existed, it would have been necessary to invent him.) If they stay and try to accomplish things in the Midwest, friends and neighbors will look at them funny. *If you're so great*, the looks will say, *why are you still here?*

After awhile, it gets weird. After awhile, even those of us in love with the likes of Cleveland find ourselves writing every word of an article like this while overlooking a backyard filled with dogwoods, magnolias, live oaks, and kudzu.